Michael
Schwartzentruber

from Crisis to New Creation

Wood Lake Books Inc.

Credits:
Cover art and illustrations: Marianne Bird
Editing: Jim Taylor
Typesetting: Kari Milton

Canadian Cataloguing in Publication Data
Schwartzentruber, Michael, 1960—
  From crisis to new creation

  ISBN 0-919599-35-4
  1. Schwartzentruber, Michael, 1960—
Christian biography - Canada. 3. Cystic
fibrosis - Patients - Canada - Biography.
I. Title.
BR1725.S39A3 1986   248.8'6'0924   C86-091395-3

Published in cooperation with
Handicapped Ministries, Mennonite Central Committee (Ontario)
by:
Wood Lake Books, Inc.
Box 700
Winfield, BC, V0H 2C0

Printed in Canada by:
Friesen Printers
Altona, MB, R0G 0B0

To Jan

I think of your love, and I am humbled.

Acknowledgments

I owe a debt of gratitude and thanks to the many people and organizations who helped make this book a reality: to Warden Woods Church and Community Centre, for the use of its word processor; to Muriel Bechtel, for her hours spent editing the initial draft—her prodding and encouragement were invaluable; to John Bender, Aldred H. Neufeldt, Mary Brubacker and Evelyn Bauer, who also read the manuscript and shared the fruits of their experience, knowledge, and expertise; to Jim Hunsberger for his unbridled enthusiasm and promotion of this project; to Mennonite Central Committee (Ontario), for establishing a fund to receive charitable donations in financial support of the book, and to all those people who made donations; to Ralph Milton and Jim Taylor, for seeing potential in the manuscript, sound advice and editing; and to Marianne Bird for her illustrations.

Finally, I owe thanks, and so much more, to my family and especially my wife Jan, for their patience, love and encouragement.

Contents

Foreword

When we pray the familiar words of the Lord's Prayer, we
affirm our dependence on a power greater than ourselves:
    Hallowed be your name,
    Your Kingdom come,
    Your will be done,
    On earth as it is in heaven.
    Give us this day our daily bread . . . .
When we pray this prayer, we give up notions of wanting to be
independent, and we express our love for God and for others.

In this book, Michael Schwartzentruber unlocks his life, in a
similar kind of prayer. He allows us to be part of the trying
experience of living with cystic fibrosis, as he learns to
overcome the constant spectre of death, to hallow God, to be
dependent on others, and to be led out of the very human temptations of anger, withdrawal, and rebellion.

You will be moved by his deliberate and honest description of
the circumstances of his life. And though you may not have
cystic fibrosis, I am sure you will identify with his struggles. It
will heighten your appreciation of interdependency, and you will
feel a one-ness with him.

Michael enables us to experience a debilitating and ultimately
terminal disease as a means of progressively gaining identity and
purpose as children of a loving and suffering God. He brings us

face to face with disability and brokenness. He challenges us to ponder penetrating questions about the universal weakness we all know. For who is not disabled? We all are disabled in some way. Not one body can claim complete physical, mental, emotional, and spiritual wholeness. This book inspires all of us to accept more honestly and openly our many vulnerabilities.

It offers us a new kind of strength, a strength found in weakness. As we accept our human limitations, we can open up to opportunities for celebrating God's love and power. This book, in a unique way, frees us. The power of God's love enables us to embrace suffering with joy, pain with laughter, realism with idealism.

On a personal note, I, like Michael, was born into this world and labelled as disabled. Cerebral palsy has been part of my life for more than 40 years. I found myself deeply touched by Michael's words, which became very real and living to me. His candor mirrors and reflects many episodes of soul-searching and spiritual struggle in my own life.

So it is with enthusiasm and delight that I recommend this book. It speaks vividly to me about concerns of accepting disability, concerns which I deal with every day, both for myself, and for those with whom I work in the Mennonite Central Committee's Handicapped Ministries.

But beyond that, this book offers an opportunity for all kinds of people to study and encounter disability. In its intimacy, this book sets an example which will, I hope, encourage others to contribute to the health of the whole church by sharing their own struggles and experiences.

Jim Hunsberger,
Coordinator, Handicapped Ministries,
Mennonite Central Committee (Ontario).

Preface

A book like this represents many things. But right now it seems easier, and just as important, to say what it is not. Though I write as one who has Cystic Fibrosis (CF), this is not a story about CF. It is, rather, the story of how I have dealt physically, emotionally, and spiritually, with the realization that I am not all I would like to be.

At times, in reading this book, you may have a feeling that I am doing a lot of talking about myself. There's a simple reason for that. It's my life that is slowly but inexorably coming to an end.

Living with the sure knowledge of your own mortality—as I have done since I was 14—gives an urgency, a unique incentive, to examine your life and make some meaning and purpose out of it. And so I write about the meaning and purpose I have discovered in my life, because it's the only life I know.

Now, there are things about myself, my life, I would change if I could. But there are also things I would not change. This book represents my effort to discern all that I am, and all I can become. It represents my attempt to find meaning and hope in life, and a healing faith in God.

As such, on one level I am writing for myself. Writing has been an effort of self-discovery and interpretation. It has been an attempt to make sense of my experience, my life.

But I am also writing with specific people in mind. This book is a way of explaining, not excusing, to my wife, my parents, and my sisters, why I have or have not done things which seem important.

I am also writing for my nephew, now eight years old, who suffers from a rare and disabling skin disease. I hope that if he reads this ten years from now, it will help him as *he* tries to make sense of his life, past, present, and future.

And ultimately, I am writing for everyone, because all of us are "disabled." Even if not physically or mentally disabled, few can claim to be emotionally or spiritually whole persons. None of us are all that we would like to be. We are all scarred by failure, rejection, doubt, and death. I write for those who have known joy, laughter, and fulfilment, as well as suffering, pain, and death. And that, I think, is just about everyone.

Finally, I have written in the hope that we may all more keenly recognize the strength which grows from weakness.

Deja vu

CHAPTER ONE

Wednesday, September 14. 6:30 a.m.

I had begun to believe that I had reached a point of equilibrium in my life; I had begun to believe that things were going to start falling into place. The day, Wednesday, September 14, started so typically, at 6:30 a.m.

The clock radio blares. Deftly, I reach out from under the bed sheets. My finger hits the "snooze" button, killing the music before the orchestra makes it to the second bar. I do it again every ten minutes, at 6:40, 6:50, and again at 7:00. Some people have a hard time getting out of bed on Monday mornings. I don't understand why getting out of bed on Mondays should be harder than any other morning. I dislike getting out of bed no matter which day of the week it is.

Although it is the first week of classes, in my first year at the University of Toronto, the prospect of newness in itself fails to make the morning procedure any more alluring. It does, however, provide *a* reason for getting out of bed.

I pat Jan three times on whatever part of her anatomy is close at hand, as a signal of my intent to get out of bed. She responds with three pats, acknowledging that she has received and understood the message. She prepares for my imminent departure by rolling over and pulling the covers up further over her head.

Having somehow achieved a sitting position, and after pulling on a pair of pants, I stumble the thirteen step distance between the bed and the bathroom. Much to Jan's chagrin, after one and a half years of marriage, I continue to display an inability to understand the precise purpose of our laundry hamper. My dirty clothes are therefore sometimes on top of it, sometimes around its base, but almost never *in* it. A successful crossing of the floor thus requires both agile footwork and keen desire. The sight of myself in the bathroom mirror is seldom pretty, so I do not linger. I pick up my equipment and proceed to the kitchen where I mix the ingredients for my morning inhalation treatment for cystic fibrosis.

Twice a day, every day, I have to inhale a fine mist of medications. My life depends on it.

Having cystic fibrosis and having to follow the daily treatment regime doesn't bother me now nearly as much as it used to. Actually, it all becomes very routine after a while, part of everyday life. The mucus which my body produces to coat and protect the lungs is simply thicker than the mucus a healthy body produces. As well, the lungs and bronchial tubes of a healthy person have little hairs called cilia, which are always moving with a waving action. These waving hairs keep moving the mucus up and out of the lungs. In a person with cystic fibrosis, the cilia don't work. The result is that the mucus, which is too thick and sticky to begin with, accumulates in the lungs, and blocks the air passages making breathing difficult.

The inhalation therapy is the first part of a two-part therapy routine, which we must do each morning and evening. I inhale a fine mist containing a drug which dilates the bronchial tubes, opening the air passages in my lungs.

The second part of the therapy routine, postural drainage, represents modern medicine's answer to the problem of mucus buildup in the lungs. You simply pound it out of the person. I have a padded board which can be set up a various angles, one end on the floor, the other end raised. I lie on this board in five different positions, most of them head down. In each position, Jan hits, with a cupped hand, a different area of my chest. The internal vibration loosens the mucus in that area of the lung.

After each position, I must sit up and cough out the mucus. The entire procedure, both the inhalation therapy and the postural drainage, takes an hour, or slightly more, to complete.

This morning things progress much as usual. Jan rolls out of bed and showers while I inhale the medicated mist. By the time I am finished, she has made coffee and is sitting on the couch watching "Canada AM." I set up my sloped postural drainage board in front of her. We begin the pounding session.

After finishing the first position, however, I suspect I should have stayed in bed. What I cough up looks unsettlingly like ketchup in consistency and color. Now I know that coughing up large amounts of blood is something one would like to avoid. On the other hand, there isn't much I can do about it. It's difficult to put a bandaid on a ruptured blood vessel inside the lung.

Jan is worried. She worked as a nurse before taking seminary training. Apparently they taught her, in nurses' training, that coughing up blood is not a good thing. My attempts to put her at ease by pointing out that the bleeding usually stops seem to have little effect. This time, the bleeding does *not* stop.

Jan is now more than worried. She suggests that I call the hospital. I am concerned as well. But calling the hospital? Nine times out of ten the doctors will want to have you admitted. Maybe ten times out of ten. Nobody goes to the hospital on the first day of university classes.

I'm not sure whether we reached agreement on the matter or whether there was simply no further discussion. I suspect the latter to be the case. Anyway, I did not call the hospital. And after breakfast Jan went to work and I went to classes.

Wednesday was a long day for me. Classes ran from 11 to 7. The subway ride took an hour. I am not a high energy person at the best of times, so I was exhausted by the time I got home. During the evening therapy session I was still coughing up blood. This time I agreed with Jan that I needed to call the hospital, but in the morning.

Thursday, September 15.
The receptionist at the hospital CF clinic said the doctors

would not be in clinic until the afternoon. Could we come then?

Jan called work to say she was taking me to the hospital. We said little during the ride to the hospital. I was sure the doctors would want to admit me. Jan tried to sound optimistic. "Maybe they'll just give you another antibiotic and send you home," she said. Experience told me not to hope for such an easy solution.

The thought of being hospitalized depressed me. I had entered the year with a certain reserved enthusiasm that comes from a change in schools and from the prospect of new courses and different professors. The enthusiasm came from a new but also unsure beginning. Hospitalization seemed an old ending.

The last time I was hospitalized was before I had met Jan. In fact, it had been five years since I had last "been in." That time I was really quite sick and for a while it appeared touch and go, whether I would survive. I was then living in London, Ontario, with my parents. I had just finished high school and had started a wonderful job. My boss kept my position open while I was hospitalized. As it turned out, I worked with him for three years. Toward the end of this period I met Jan. She was a seminary student at Elkhart, Indiana, in London for a year as a pastoral intern in my home congregation.

On her first pastoral visit to our family, she and I discovered a common interest in jazz. One thing led to another. By the end of her intern year in London we had decided we wanted to get married, but not for another year. Jan returned to her studies in Elkhart, and I decided to go back to school, majoring in Religious Studies. I enrolled in a church college in Winnipeg, affiliated with the University of Manitoba. The following June, Jan and I were married in Indiana. Jan had one more year of seminary to complete, so we stayed in Elkhart. I was accepted at her seminary as a special student for one year.

Our first year of marriage had its ups and downs but it was good to be in school, especially since it would probably be the last chance we would have to be students together.

We planned to return to Ontario after Jan's final year, as staying in the United States would have meant giving up my Canadian health insurance.

Without Canadian "medicare," I couldn't afford to keep on

living. My prescribed drugs alone would cost $4000 or so every year—and that's when they're picked up "at cost" at the hospital. Purchased in the conventional way at a drug store, I'm sure they would have cost twice as much.

In the U.S., too, I would have to pay for hospitalization. My last time, in London, I was "in" for 14 days, the minimum time needed for intravenous antibiotic treatment against the bacteria that delight in the warm, moist mucus they find in my lungs. At $800 or more a day, that one stay would have set me $11,000 into debt. In Canada, it cost me nothing—except time and frustration.

Jan found a job in Scarborough, Ontario, where we took up residence in June. I applied that summer to the University of Toronto and, much to my pleasure, was accepted.

As the subway rolled out of the station where I would have gotten off to attend classes, and headed on towards the hospital, I had to reflect on how good the last five years had been, and how much I held to the hope of another equally meaningful five years. At that moment, I did not interpret being sick and on the way to the hospital as a step in the right direction.

Consultation with the doctor confirmed my fears.

I was struck by a profound sense of deja vu as Jan and I passed through the hallway doors and entered Ward 7E. I had not been on this cystic fibrosis ward, or even in this hospital, since I was ten years old, because my family had moved from Toronto to London in 1970.

Now I was back. Though it was still afternoon, the overhead lights in the hallway of the ward were turned off; only the nurses station about half way down the hall was brightly illuminated. The effect added an eeriness to my emotional discomfort.

This was where it had all begun, in terms of my own memory of CF. I couldn't help wondering if this was also where it would all end.

Why me?

CHAPTER TWO

Hospitalization on September 15, turned out to be a crisis point of a kind I have experienced at various times in my life. It has most often been during times of crisis that I have felt the need to stop, and take account of my situation, to ask who and why I am. Perhaps it's the only time one does ask such questions. Why, after all, stop for probing self-analysis when everything's going well?

Sometimes, in asking these questions, I have been startled by new insights into my situation and into myself as a person. At other times, I have reclaimed an understanding or appreciation of myself and those who are part of my life, which had slipped away when an earlier crisis had passed, and the commonplace again dominated my life.

So this hospitalization was neither an end nor a beginning for me, but was, in some measure, an event which put me back in touch with my own realities. Not that I ever forget that I have CF. I may forget where I've put my wallet and keys, but never CF. The twice daily therapy routine prohibits forgetting. And yet, after a period of months and now years of health, having CF becomes to some extent just that—routine. Therapy is simply a part of my life. Even the tightness in my chest, the difficulty breathing, although I am always aware of it, somehow blends into the background of daily living and becomes a natural part of it.

The day-to-day living of the last five years had been going so well. Jan and I were married. Marriage was something I had hoped for but which also seemed somehow beyond hope for a permanently ill person. My return to school had been, and I hoped would continue to be, a happy and meaningful experience. Hospitalization was the the shock. It brought back the sense of uniqueness and seriousness of living with CF, an incurable and usually terminal condition. The thought, "I *am* disabled," returned with force.

I have found the occasional sudden re-recognition of the fact that I am disabled almost as unsettling as the first time it really embedded itself in my consciousness. I have often wondered what it must be like to be told after thirty-five years of good health, that cancer has been found in your body. Surely, I've thought, that must be more traumatic than growing up and living with a disease that you've always known was a part of you. Maybe it is. Yet I think there is a point of sudden recognition even for those who have had a handicap from birth. Images of therapy treatments are imprinted upon even earliest childhood memories. But the understanding of the child is not the understanding of the adult.

When I was eight years old, having to stay in the house and do therapy before being allowed to go out and play was mostly a matter of irritation and frustration, at times worthy of tears. No doubt my parents received the brunt of my displeasure. They were, after all, the authority figures perpetrating this massive plot to spoil my fun. The thought that therapy might represent something other than a restriction of my desire to ride my bicycle did not occur to me.

Even when I was somewhat older, and able to start thinking from a longer-term perspective, the realities of living with a severe illness did not strike with any personal force. I remember several discussions with thirteen-year-old peers during which I calmly outlined the nature of my illness, including the recognition that my life expectancy was only twenty-five to thirty years. Although I understood that what I was saying was serious, it felt more like playing a game. I enjoyed the air of maturity I thought such pronouncements lent me. I was mouthing words which had only marginal personal impact.

The crisis came a year or so later, when I was fourteen. I had gone to the CF clinic for my regular three-month check-up. Chest X-rays revealed a growing lung deterioration. When the mucus that forms in the tiny passages of the lungs isn't dislodged by regular therapy, it clogs. Parts of the lungs get blocked off. Inevitably, those parts die. Starved for oxygen, they begin to look, and act, like leather instead of healthy lung tissue.

I had not, up to that point, been doing therapy on a very regular or adequate basis. When I was younger, my physical condition was not so advanced that my health suffered from skipping therapy occasionally or from doing it only once a day. Often I would skip therapy altogether on the weekends. Like many who are much older then me, intellectually and verbally I knew that my condition was slowly deteriorating, and would continue to do so. Emotionally, however, I had not yet dealt with or accepted the fact of my mortality. As a result, the lifestyle changes that would be necessary to maintain my health did not seem worth the cost.

But on this occasion, the doctor was concerned enough to sit a fourteen-year-old down and explain rather sternly that I had to start doing therapy regularly, because "from here on it's all downhill."

I was stunned; and I wasn't sure why. I would have been able to say the doctor's words about myself, to anyone who might have asked. But the words I spoke or heard before had been merely words. The reality—for which the words had only been symbols—had never really touched my sense of being. Now here I was, like my peers, just beginning to discover a life full of possibilities and the self-confidence to pursue them, confronting the words "from here on it's all downhill."

I shall be forever grateful for this man's honesty and concern. Some feel that a doctor should never say such a thing to a patient, especially one so young. I disagree. An honest picture of my situation was the only position from which I could come to grips with reality and make meaningful decisions. Honesty is something we *all* need and deserve. It was something I needed.

Honesty is essential, but it can also be painful. With the shock of recognition came a period of anger and depression. I remember asking many "Why me?" questions of God. Why me? What had I ever done to deserve this? What hadn't I done? Why are you picking on me, God?

It seems strange to me now that I was asking those questions. I had, at that point in my life, not made any kind of faith commitment. I was not even sure God really existed, or at least I hadn't openly admitted it to myself or anyone else. Yet all my questioning presupposed, or presumed, God's presence.

Maybe I was just looking for someone on whom to blame my problems. God obviously had it in for me. Or, if it wasn't God, it was that elusive character, Fate. Or it was someone or something else. Whoever, whatever, my situation was definitely not a result of my own doing.

Ten years have passed and I have yet to find a satisfactory answer to the question "Why me?" I guess I'm no longer sure there is any answer to that question.

What if there were an answer? What if I had been able to sit down face-to-face with God and have it out? What if God had said, "Yes, Mike, there is a reason, which is . . . ." Then what would I have done? Would it really have helped me to be less angry, less hurt, less broken? Could I, would I, have accepted the answer? Would any of us?

Sometimes, as I have struggled with this concern, I have found a provocative parallel in an incident during World War II. The British captured a German "enigma" machine used to send coded messages. Through the use of this machine, the British were able to break German codes and thereby sometimes learn of impending attacks. On one such occasion, the British intercepted a German communique which detailed a planned air strike on the English city of Coventry.

British Intelligence was in a quandary. If they alerted and evacuated the city, the Germans would guess that the British had broken their codes. If they did not warn the city, thousands of innocent people would probably be killed. But the fact that they had broken the German codes would remain hidden, possibly helping to bring an earlier end to the war.

British Intelligence did not alert the city. Many people were killed. Almost certainly, those who lost loved ones as a result of the bombing asked themselves and their leaders why it had to be. I wonder if the fact that Britain's leaders were able to provide an explanation, a "why," helped the grieving families? Maybe, if they were very patriotic, they could understand and possibly even agree with the reasoning behind the decision. But I wonder if knowing or even agreeing helped to heal the hurt, helped to fill the sense of loss.

And what if surviving family and friends did *not* agree with the decision?

What if God really had an answer to my "Why me?" question? What if God said, "Mike, suffering is an integral part of my plan for salvation"? What if I couldn't believe in a God who allowed, or worse, planned for such suffering? Then what?

And what if I could have had the conversation with God, and received an answer that I *could* live with. Somehow I suspect the pain and hurt resulting from my lost health, my lost wholeness would remain.

The cry, "God, why me?" still echoes in the empty stillness of my soul. And slowly, so slowly, I realize that an explanation is not what I want. I want to be comforted, consoled. I want God and the people in my life to know that I hurt. I want to be loved, held. I want something to fill the emptiness my loss has left within me.

That understanding has dawned only years after my initial shock at age fourteen. During those first months of anger, my desire to be loved and accepted by God was not something I could or would admit. I was, however, able to reach a temporary peace.

As I slowly worked my way down the street, delivering newspapers on that grey and cold November day ten years ago, I asked the question "Why me?" for the umpteenth time and finally arrived at an answer. Why *not* me? It wasn't very profound, perhaps, but it at least held potential for greater future understanding and acceptance. It was, at least, an admission that if I didn't know why this happened to me, I also didn't know why it shouldn't have happened to me, as opposed to someone else. One in every 2,000 babies is born with CF. In the great lottery of life, my number had obviously come up.

My first "answer" at least helped me realize that God was not out to get me. God was not venting anger upon me for something I had done or not done. The realization that God was not angry with me, in turn, allowed me to be less angry with God. As a result, I began to feel a greater closeness to God, and was more able to listen for God's "still small voice."

Thus my initial crisis led me to re-evaluate my relationships with the people in my life, and to God. It led to a recognition that my relationships required constant review and strengthening. It challenged me to seek meaning in life, and to live meaningfully.

Each new hospitalization since then has pushed me to continue the process.

Understanding and acceptance of my disability is not something which has occurred in a momentary flash of insight. Acceptance of my mortality has been a long process of growth. It will continue to be part of my life process as I grow and change in character and situation.

The tacit acceptance that I was dying, an acceptance which I first began to reach after the initial shock at age fourteen, was but one step in a long journey. That journey is still in progress for me—as it is for each and every human. The shock of recognition hit me again at age sixteen, and at eighteen, and at twenty-two, and now again at twenty-three. Each time I met a crisis it forced me to re-evaluate myself as an individual, as a person in relation to those around me, and as a being in relation to God. Each time the anger, resentment, and some of the doubts brought out by earlier crises, have re-emerged. The direction of my questioning has differed, but the basic ingredients were always present. Truth always takes time to sink in.

Two years after my doctor's revelation, I still was not taking very good care of myself. As a result I was hospitalized with a chest infection. At that point, for the first time, I really accepted my condition and started making definite life-style changes. I decreased my school work load, and did therapy twice a day, *every* day.

Two years after that I was again hospitalized. At that point, I was struggling with issues of autonomy and family relations. Later, marriage again changed my situation and again I had to re-evaluate old relationships and commitments. I had to discover what my handicap, my decreased life expectancy, meant in the new setting of marriage to Jan.

It has been during these times of crisis that recognition and acceptance of my identity as a person—disabled, but even in that a person like all others—has come. Sometimes this new awareness has faded with my return to the routines of daily living.

Yet with each new crisis, I have been able to stretch my awareness, to reach new understanding. With each return to "normalcy" I have retained more of the hard-won insight, acceptance, and peace I ultimately seek. Despite not wanting to be there, I knew that my current stay in the hospital was likely to produce its own benefits.

Robert Redford's foot

CHAPTER THREE

The first thing you lose after being admitted to a hospital is your dignity. Hospital procedures and practices notoriously violate the privacy of many otherwise inviolate body parts and functions.

I tend to be a well-behaved patient. But several days after I had settled in, the young and attractive female resident in charge of my care, who had previously shown me no ill-will, announced that I was to begin a three day stool collection. I didn't take it too personally since she bore the same good tidings to my equally—more or less—well-behaved roommate a minute later.

I have never really been able to understand doctors. *I* collected stamps for many years, only recently forgoing that fine hobby. Many people I know have entertained other varied but equally respectable collecting interests. But doctors? Doctors collect *stool* specimens.

My roomie and I were provided with shiny new one-gallon cans into which we were to deposit our contributions to the doctors' somewhat questionable collecting interests. The tin cans were stored in a greatly overheated "cubbyhole," a kind of broom closet, about three doors down the hall from our room. Within the storage room was a small, almost adequately functioning refrigerator in which we were to place the cans when not in use. The refrigerator was efficient enough to render the cans cold to the touch—especially from the rear. But it was not cold enough to greatly diminish unappreciated odors, whose potency grew remarkably over the three-day aging process.

The room's overactive heating system further enhanced the aroma. It did not enhance our sense of dignity. Depositing samples became a malodorous task, in the fullest possible sense of the word. The presence of our collections made itself known to anyone travelling our stretch of hallway, which meant almost everyone on the ward.

My roommate and I spent much time commiserating upon our lot in life. We began to suspect that we were destined to become complete social outcasts. Needless to say, we were both quite relieved when the end of the third day arrived.

Although there is no place I would rather be when I am sick or in need of extra medical care, the life of a hospital patient is obviously fraught with many potential risks to personal dignity and self-image.

For a chronically disabled person, however, questions of self-image arise not only during times of crisis, or under special circumstances such as hospitalization. They are likely to be daily concerns.

In a fast paced society which gives little time to developing relationships, first impressions carry a lot of weight. As a result, most of us like to put our best foot forward.

We each have our weaknesses which we prefer to keep hidden until we feel secure enough in a situation or relationship to reveal that part of ourselves to others. But for many people with a disability, "putting your best foot forward" is simply not possible, using society's concept of "best foot." Many—especially those with visible physical difficulties—simply don't have the luxury of concealing their "shortcomings" until they feel comfortable in a relationship. Too often, what others may consider a weakness is too obvious to hide.

I am lucky. My disability presents few obvious external characteristics. Some people who have known me for a period of time have later been surprised to learn I have CF. Like the person who is able to hide what he or she may consider a foible, I can usually control encounters with new people so that having CF remains concealed.

However, this is not always the case. My decision to leave home and to go back to school and live in residence, was just such a situation. I applied to the Canadian Mennonite Bible College in Winnipeg, because it offered the kind of undergraduate theological education I desired. As I require help with my postural drainage, it was necessary, upon my initial application to request the aid of other students. The college registrar thought this would not pose a problem and felt such assistance could easily be arranged. His reassurances did little to alleviate my uneasiness. While living at home, my parents had provided the help I required. Although my friends had often watched and occasionally helped, I had never had to depend on them. If they helped, it was by my choice, my initiative. Being forced to give up that control, by a mere shift in my living environment, was unsettling.

I remember sitting under a shade tree with Jan, then my fiancee, two weeks before the start of school. I expressed to her my anxiety about the impending move. I would have to meet these people, and on the very first day, before they had a chance to get to know me or I them, they would have to be instructed in the fine art of postural drainage. They would watch and listen while I coughed up the mucus from my chest. I worried about having to so blatantly and quickly expose my weaker self. I shared my fear that they would find me repulsive. I remember sitting back and saying, "Well, I guess I have fourteen days to come to terms with this."

Jan suggested that maybe I should give myself more time. Was it not asking too much of myself, to expect that I could fully deal with such issues in so short a time? Some people never manage to deal with them in a lifetime. I would, she said wisely, be working with these issues for a long time.

She was right, of course. But she also missed the point—at least the point I was trying to make. I was giving myself fourteen days to get over my fear of such personal exposure, because that exposure was going to occur then, whether I was emotionally ready to deal with it or not. For people with a disability, facing a world which may or may not accept us as we are is something we can't postpone until we're comfortable with ourselves, or until the world is comfortable with us. It is something we must face every time we leave secure and familiar surroundings or enter into new relationships.

As it turned out, anticipating the adjustment to dorm life was worse than the reality. The admissions counselor and I decided that since I required the aid of another person for an hour and a half each day, seven different people should be chosen to assist me. Each person would be responsible for a specific day, so that the time demands upon any one person would not be too great. The system worked well. It also held some benefits I had not considered. Having a number of people who were informed about and involved with my treatment meant that fairly accurate information about my condition could be disseminated quickly, without my necessarily having to answer all the questions myself. More importantly, although I tend to be a quiet person and make friends slowly, here in my new surroundings I now had at least seven people who quickly became friends with whom I could talk.

In the end I discovered, as I had on other occasions, an acceptance and friendship which was not hampered, but rather enhanced as we shared my handicap.

The experience reinforced for me a basic, and paradoxical, truth of the Scriptures. Jesus often talked in paradoxes, about losing one's life to gain it, for example, or about real strength being found in weakness and vulnerability. I have found that to be true in my own life. Our society takes for granted that strength derives from rugged independence, and that weakness or dependence is somehow to be avoided. Yet when I entered that college residence, I found that my weakness, my dependence, became an unexpected asset. Those who volunteered to help me, shared in my handicap in the sense that they committed themselves to working with me on a schedule and in a manner determined by the handicap itself. Also, the stress of living with a handicap was shared, in that greater mutual trust and acceptance was necessary for the initiation and maintenance of our relationship.

I still want to put my best foot forward. Yet, if my inability to present an image of the ideal, whole person, has forced me to turn to others with greater openness and trust, maybe I have already put my best foot forward.

The desire to be accepted by others, the effort to put my best foot forward, represents only half my self-image dilemma. The other half is my desire that it be Robert Redford's foot.

The tensions and anxieties I experience when initiating new relationships are truly minor compared to those I create for myself. Like everyone else, perhaps, I have some questionable ideals of perfection. Perfection, a la Michael Schwartzentruber, has included a desire to enroll in six courses at school, get straight A's, be a helpful husband, and write a book or two on the side. The tension arises when my "selves," the ideal and the actual, meet—or rather, fail to meet.

My inner dialogue usually starts with the preamble, "if only I were healthy . . . ," and quickly moves on to any of the following assertions: ". . . I would take six courses," (a full load is five), ". . . I would get straight A's," ". . . I would be a wonderful husband . . . ."

You know how it goes. You may not preface your statements with "If I were healthy . . . ." You may say, "If I were rich . . ." or "If I had more time . . ." or even "If I believed that . . ." but the principle is the same.

The problems with this kind of idealizing start with the fact that not everyone else takes six courses, gets straight A's, or is a perfect husband, even with good health. That's something my "If . . ." projections seem prone to forget. This projection of perfection also ignores other limitations. I might not have the scholastic aptitude to take six courses and get straight A's, even if I had the physical energy or stamina to attempt such a feat. But the ideal image stands nonetheless. It is only natural, I suppose, since few people are satisfied with who they are. But natural or not, the failure to live up to my imagined ideal is painful.

And that pain is only multiplied as the gap between my ideal self and the reality widens. Said another way: coping with the desire to be perfect is one thing, but when you're on a downhill slide it is quite another.

When I started school in Winnipeg, I felt well enough to take a full five-course load. In the following years, as my health and energy declined, I dropped to four courses, and then to three.

Now, here I am, in hospital, with both school work and my commitments to Jan and our home life suffering because there seems to be less and less of me to spread around. The unpleasant prospect of cutting back even further looms large. I find myself realizing that I was doing well when I took four courses, and wishing that I could just return to that level. If only . . . .

Realizing and accepting that one has limited energies, and then deciding how and where those energies will be spent, is a painful process. Jan, my parents, people close to me, have tried to make such choices easier for me. "What's so important about finishing your degree?" they say. "You enjoy being a student. That's the important thing. Take as many courses as you have energy for. Don't worry about the degree. There's no hurry."

Their response to my desire to achieve as many A's as possible is usually similar. "Why tire yourself out working so hard for an A? Why not be satisfied with B's and C's and have energy left for other things?"

In my head I know they are right, but in the midst of the turmoil that I experience, their attempts to make my decisions easier leave me feeling cold. It almost seems as though I'm not supposed to have the same kinds of goals and aspirations I see other people possessing. It seems as if everyone else is encouraged to work hard and take pride in their achievements, to feel satisfaction at having done something well. But not me. Because I have a disability, I should be willing to compromise my standards.

Again, I know that this is not what Jan and my parents mean or intend at all. And yet, that is how I often feel.

It wasn't until I began to understand my turmoil and pain as a valid grief response, to a very real loss, that I understood my angry reaction to people's attempts to help me accept and see the positive value of my choices. Telling someone whose house has just burned down that they should be glad that no one was killed may be a true statement. But it will appear to minimize their loss and thus also the grief they are experiencing. Anger is a natural response. Anger has often been my response.

Grief has to progress at its own pace. When I'm hurting because I've had to give up something I value highly, I don't want someone telling me all the reasons why I should be thankful, or presenting all the options still open to me. I need someone to simply recognize and to share with me my pain and loss. My ability to find reasons to be thankful, and my desire to seek advice on options, will return, after I've had time to recognize and experience my loss. Acceptance can follow more freely, when I'm ready.

Having said all that, I realize that the need to reduce my course load, for instance, would not be such a traumatic affair if I didn't identify myself so completely with what I do. By equating myself with what I do or produce I create most of my own problems and tensions. I like to study and learn. I go to school. Therefore, I am a student. A neat equation. But tension arises when I have to cut back on courses. If I am less able to be a student, then I am somehow less of a person. Or at least, I am less of the person I thought I was. And thus my identity crisis.

Acceptance of who I am, of myself as a disabled person, really only begins on those rare occasions when I remember that I am first and foremost a creature loved by my Creator. My sense of who I am depends not on my limitations, physical, emotional, spiritual, but on my relationship to God. I stand before God, desperately needing and hoping for a little grace.

As a person who stands in relationship to God, as a person who is loved by God, I am of infinite worth—no matter what my personal limitations. God knows that I am a finite person with finite capabilities. But God's love is infinite, and thus my infinite value as a child of God.

Just recognizing, believing, and on occasion, even profoundly experiencing this truth, has often served as the grace I need so badly. The recognition that God loves me even when I can't seem to love myself, the recognition that God can tolerate my

shortcomings even when I cannot, is grace of a most healing
kind. Recognition and acceptance of this kind of grace has been
difficult for me. But I have experienced it, maybe not often or
predictably, maybe only during isolated moments of prayer or
quiet reflection, but I have received it. And it has been healing.

Recognition and acceptance of my limitations as a person has
also meant awareness and acceptance of the grace of God which
I have received through the people in my life. An experience I
had at seminary stands as an excellent example.

My year at seminary in Elkhart was a time of struggle. It was
only the second year of my return to formal education and I was
perhaps in over my head. It was also the first year of married
life for Jan and me, with most of the stressful adjustments that
entails. I was depressed. I was trying to come to terms with
what my limited life expectancy meant for our new marriage
relationship. And I was having only limited success.

In all of this it seemed very important to me to maintain a full
course load. By the final week of classes, it became painfully
obvious that I had not been keeping up with the work for one
course in particular. The night before the exam I was in a
panic. I did not know the material. I could not bluff my way
through by memorizing a few stock phrases. I had a headache
and felt nauseated.

Jan suggested that I talk to the professor and explain how I
was feeling and why. She encouraged me to ask for the grace
which she felt sure he could and would offer.

I did talk to the professor. He offered me more time before I
wrote the exam. But we were moving back to Canada in five
days. I explained that I no longer had the physical or emotional
energy to do the work and that an extension would only prolong
the agony and delay the inevitable. I needed out. I was prepared
to accept the notation of late withdrawal on my academic
record, even something as undesirable as an "F" stamped in
scarlet letters. What I got was understanding, acceptance, and
permission to withdraw from the course. Without notation or
academic penalty. Grace.

It is by the grace which I receive from God and through the
people in my life, that I can find the desire and strength to

continue daily living. With the acceptance I experience from God, and those with whom I live and work, comes acceptance of myself and a willingness to work within my circumstances.

Jan and my parents are right. I do enjoy going to school and find much of value in the experience. Such enjoyment and enrichment is reason enough to continue. I don't have to take five courses or finish my degree to validate either my decision to go to school or myself as a person. And although setting goals is important and helpful, I am not what I set out to do or produce. My value as a human being is not dependent upon success or failure.

Who am I? Certainly not the idealized image I often choose to create, but that I fail to achieve. Ultimately I am a child of God: all else needs to grow as a response to that truth.

One
to
another

CHAPTER FOUR

Another endless evening in the hospital. And all I really want, you know, is something to relieve the worst case of headache, post nasal drip, and sore throat that I have ever had. The decongestant doesn't have to be brought on a silver platter. Just bring it.

I know the nurses are doing the best they can. They have to wait for the doctor to write a prescription. And I know the doctor is doing the best she can. She's had five admissions in the last two hours, so it's not as though she is purposely ignoring me. But it would only take her three minutes to write out a prescription and have it sent to the hospital pharmacy.

It is just so frustrating. I asked for a decongestant three hours ago, hoping it would clear my head so I could sleep. It is now after eleven with no relief in sight. If I were at home I could have gotten out of bed, raided the medicine cabinet, and been asleep in half an hour. But here I lie, fretting. I *hate* being so dependent.

What is even more frustrating is that I still let things like this get to me. I should be used to this by now. This is not my first time in hospital. It is certainly not the first time I have felt my basic dependencies so acutely. But I really thought I had come to terms with the anger, resentment and insecurity already. I've read Erikson. I've already had my autonomy crises!

Isn't that why you become a teenager—so you can work through all this stuff and then go on and lead a normal adult life? Am I right? Why else would anyone want to be an adolescent? Looking back I can laugh about it now.

I spent half my teenage life holed away in my parents' basement. (They weren't being cruel—that's where my bedroom was.) I spent a lot of time down there, pondering what the future might hold for a person like me. In my mind's eye, it mostly held more of the same. I envisioned spending the rest of my life there. Maybe it wouldn't be so bad. My room had nice bookshelves, a display case, a stereo. What more could I want from life?

FREEDOM!

Isn't that what all normal teenagers want? It's what my friends wanted. Yes, I did have friends. By and large we were a fairly normal group, except perhaps that we generally got along well with our parents, didn't take drugs or drink and drive, and didn't have problems with our girl friends. We didn't *have* girl friends. Okay, maybe we weren't completely normal.

But we did want freedom.

And my problem—I can't speak for my friends—was that I just could not see myself progressing beyond a limited point in my bid for freedom. I just did not understand myself as being free to make the choices I saw the rest of the world making. I wanted to move away from home. But who would do my therapy? I wanted to get married. But who would be crazy enough to marry someone with CF? Someone who may not live long enough for a traditional "long and happy" marriage? Life in my basement seemed a more likely future.

So I rebelled. Perhaps not with the usual teenage flare, but I pulled off a rebellion just the same.

It was a sneak attack, really. So subtle I didn't even know I was doing it. I wasn't even aware whom I was attacking.

In the early years it just consisted of a hesitation, a reluctance, to do any more therapy than was absolutely necessary. My doctor had warned me that, from here on, it would be all downhill unless I started taking better care of myself. Yet I continued to function with quite a different notion of what was "absolutely necessary" than he did. It wasn't that I didn't do therapy. I just didn't do it often enough. Or carefully enough.

Now it is one thing to rebel against an abstract notion like dependence upon others. It is quite another to take it out on your own body. My experience has been that the human body does not suffer fools gladly. If you mistreat it, sooner or later you'll pay a price.

Fortunately, in my case my body only waited two years. That was when I found myself in hospital again. For some reason the doctor's message finally sank in. Perhaps I realized I wasn't doing anyone, least of all myself, any good by my behavior. Anyway, I dropped my first class of the day to allow time to do therapy in the morning. I also became more conscientious in my evening therapy routine. As a result I soon found myself healthier and happier than I had been for some time. I also found that therapy, at least, was one form of dependency I could live with. Or perhaps I should say, I realized that therapy was a dependency which I could not live without. Sometimes positive change comes only as a result of absolute necessity.

I must have suspected that a physical rebellion directed against my basic dependencies was doomed to failure. Like a good rebel, I had prepared a back-up plan. This one was more subtle. If I could never be physically autonomous, I could at least take care of myself intellectually. I could think for myself.

So I became the thoughtful silent type. Ideas became very important to me. They became so important that I hesitated to share my formulated ideas or even casual thoughts and impressions until I was convinced of their adequacy. Furthermore, I thought I needed to have answers to *all* my questions.

I also decided that I should be emotionally self-sustaining. I had family and friends of course. But I decided that I was not going to be ultimately dependent upon them for my emotional well-being. I would not leave that to others. I would simply go through life with a stiff upper lip.

Does any of this sound familiar? Talking about it later, at home, in church, with friends and acquaintances, I've been surprised at how many people nod and smile as they recognize themselves, too. It's made me wonder if my disability is as unique as I used to think.

My desire to be independent and self-sustaining was perhaps most evident in my struggle to find a God to whom I could relate. And all three aspects of my rebellion—physical, intellectual, and emotional—contributed to my failure to find such a God. At this time, at an age of about 16, I had not made any commitment to God. My lack of commitment was a result of decision, not neglect. I had, I thought, valid claims against God. I also had reasons why I thought entering into an intentional relationship would not be authentic.

First on my list of claims was my physical condition. I had done some thinking on the matter. I had decided that God was not "out to get me," and didn't necessarily *want* me to have CF. The disease itself was due to a combination of bad genes and bad luck, the odds being about 2,000 to 1 that any given set of parents will produce a cystic child. But now that I had lucked out and been born cystic, God did not appear to be going out of his way to do anything about it. There wasn't a miracle cure in sight.

Second came my desire for intellectual integrity. I needed answers. How could I commit myself to God when I still had not figured out why God allows suffering? And I had other questions. Is God at work in the world? If so, where? And where do I fit in? I was bound and determined to find the answers myself, *before* I made a commitment.

That attitude may reveal a common misconception endemic in today's world—that our relationship with God in some way depends on *our* initiative. That we come to God on *our* terms, having worked out answers for ourselves. Only after all that has been completed are we, by and large, willing to let God get involved.

Finally, the emotional aspect. Since God was not doing much for me physically, and as I was quite capable of answering my own intellectual questions, I didn't see why I needed a relationship with God for my emotional well-being.

Crisis has a way of crippling even the most firmly held of our illusions. A teacher of mine once said that it is when we come to the end of our rope that we are most likely to recognize truth in our situation and to experience the nearness of God.

The end of my rope came soon enough. Having just struggled through the final month of high school and a stressful two weeks on the job of my dreams, I found myself back in the hospital. For fourteen days I was spiking fevers in excess of 103 °F.

One night remains particularly vivid. I remember the darkness, the one light on in the room, the friends who had come to visit, the looks of pained concern on their faces. I remember lying awake at 3 a.m. asking God to let me die rather than continue to live like this. And I remember being afraid . . . scared to death, literally . . . .

Then abruptly, inexplicably, I knew I would live. I knew I *wanted* to live. I remember becoming aware of the nearness, love, and acceptance of God. I remember my father, sitting through the night by my bed. I remember the change of shift, my mother's arrival in the morning.

This experience gave my quest for autonomy and identity new direction. I began to understand the strength and support, the courage to continue, and the love, which I had drawn all of my life from the people around me. And I began to recognize God's hand in that love. I began to comprehend the ways and the extent to which God *had* been sustaining me all these years. In my search for a God to whom *I* could be faithful, I was ultimately confronted by the absolute faithfulness *of God.*

In that moment, I became aware of that pervasive misconception I mentioned earlier. It wasn't up to me after all. I wasn't alone, because God could take the initiative in our relationship.

With that recognition, autonomy and identity began to take on new meaning. I began to understand that my hope for autonomy is inherently linked to my identity as a child of God, as someone created by the Creator. I had to stop thinking of myself as an independent, isolated being with no need of the Creator, a being solely responsible for my own existence, if not for *all* existence.

I began to realize that my notion of autonomy could and should include free thinking openness to God, and the freedom

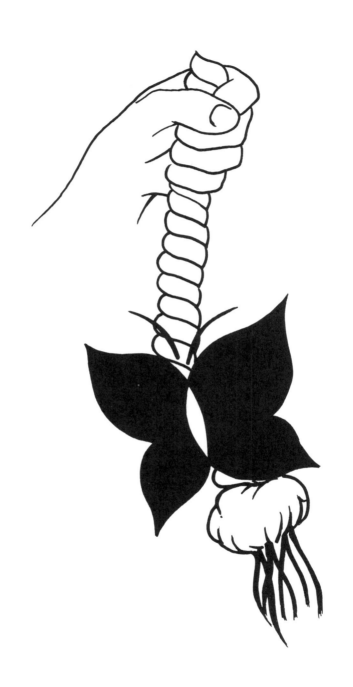

to recognize and accept the natural interdependencies we all
share, one to another, and all to God, by virtue of
our humanity.

My attempt to understand God took new direction. The questions I had asked of God had been the biggest obstacle in my
path, not *because* I asked them, but because of the *way* I asked
and sought to answer them.

First, I had to admit that I would never answer all of my
questions. I would, no doubt, go to my grave asking questions.

Second, 'and it seems so obvious now, the only way to answer
questions of faith is from a position of faith. If I needed to be
convinced that God is active in the world, I had first to accept
in faith that God *IS*. Where and how God is at work is visible
most clearly to the ''faithed'' eye.

Third, if I was ever to understand God in any measure it
would not be because *I* had figured out God. It would not be
solely the result of my brain power. Rather, understanding of
God would result from reflection upon *God,* revealed voluntarily
and freely in the lives and world around me.

To say that this experience changed my life would be true.
Life did change. I experienced more warmth, mutual support,
and love, all around. Eventually I went back to school. I got
married. Many things I had never expected to be part of my life
were suddenly mine. But my problems did not all come to an
end. The problems continued, because I am still a better
theoretician than practician.

My marriage offers a good example.

No doubt for most people the first year of marriage poses a
genuine challenge to their idealistic theories about married life.
You know, all those ideas about how different it would be after
you got married, and how you would relate in marriage. It
should be a better publicized fact that people are qualified to be
experts on marriage only so long as they remain unmarried.

Now I never claimed to possess a great theory on marriage. I
did, however, enter our marriage relationship armed with my
relatively new and largely untested theories about the merits of
intimacy and mutual dependence.

I had also, I thought, entered marriage having already worked through most of the pain and anger I had experienced at the prospect of my shortened life expectancy. To make matters worse, I assumed that Jan thought so too. But the relationship in which Jan and I now found ourselves provided a whole new context in which I had to try to reorient my old perceptions and feelings about death.

It is strange how some of our most profound theoretical insights abandon us in the face of practical exposure. As old feelings of anger, insecurity, and resentment returned, so did my old ways of dealing with them. I found it very difficult to share my feelings with Jan. I withdrew and became depressed. I had to have answers and I had to find them myself. I asked many questions of God, but did very little listening. I would not let Jan participate in my search. I would not even let her know that I was lost and desperate for answers, because I thought she expected me to have them already.

Ah, the foolishness of inexperience. I was quite taken aback when Jan later revealed that she knew I was depressed, and that she never, ever, not even once, thought that I had all the answers.

Fortunately time is a marvelous healer. Some marital counseling didn't hurt either. And again I found that together, and with the help of others, we could face what I could no longer face alone.

The theory was correct. But finding the strength to overcome old defenses and actually live it was not, and is not, that easy. It never is.

And that might also be the reason why I lie here in bed, fuming because I can not find a nurse who can find a doctor who can find me a decongestant. They say practice makes perfect. I think being hospitalized makes me so acutely aware of my dependencies that I can not ignore them. Such forced awareness of my limitations still hurts. Perhaps all I need to recognize right now is that growth is not only continuous, but often painful.

Half
the
battle

CHAPTER FIVE

I must confess that I harbor a definite dislike of dieticians. It is nothing personal. I'm sure most of them are pleasant people whom I would like, if I met them at a party. Unfortunately, I have never met one at a party. Rather, I keep bumping into them in hospital, and the resulting bruises to my sense of self and ego are enough to keep my prejudices—if not by body— well fed.

Now I have no idea what a dietician would talk about at a party. But this afternoon, with a dietician standing at the foot of my bed, the conversation is predictable. Specifically, the issue is food; what kind, how much, and will I eat it.

In the body of a person with CF, the same thick mucus found in the lungs also blocks the passage of digestive enzymes from the pancreas to the intestines. This lack is made up—but only in part—by taking enzymes in an oral capsule form. Some of the nutritional value of food eaten is still lost. And although some people with CF have voracious appetites, others have poor appetites. Many therefore suffer from varying degrees of malnutrition.

A high fat, high protein, high calorie, diet is the answer. Some adult patients are even prescribed two beer a day to add some calories and fat. After all, maintaining proper body weight *is* important in fighting any illness. Thus, the seemingly singlemindedness of the dietician's train of thought.

A food fixation is, I suppose, no great sin especially if the person's job requires it. But I do not have a food fixation. I do not derive any great pleasure from eating. I never have and I probably never will. If there were some way to go through life without the bother of eating I would know about it. I have only a moderate appetite, so eating takes an inordinate effort.

But I do eat. I just do not enjoy it much. I therefore dislike being told what to eat. I detest being told how much to eat. And I no doubt become totally irrational when someone openly plots new ways to entice me—force me, to my way of thinking—to eat more.

You see, it is not the dieticians' fault at all. They just do their job. I am the one with the hang-up.

I think what really irritates me most about dieticians is that they _know_ I am the one with the problem. They know I am the one who gets irrational at times. Even worse, they have so many annoying ways of letting me know they know.

Like the one who came to see me this afternoon. He informed me that my failure to gain weight was now of prime concern to everyone except, apparently, myself. He obviously was not interested in becoming friends. And he was wrong, partially.

I _know_ that I am underweight and I _do_ acknowledge that as being a legitimate concern. But after years of maintaining a stable weight, I have difficulty convincing myself that a failure to gain a few kilograms represents any kind of crisis. So, I admit concern, but do not share it to his degree.

To make matters worse, he continued by appealing to my sense of reason and responsibility—a dangerous tactic when dealing with an angry person. "Being underweight operates against your general well-being," he said. "You are married so your responsibilities include your wife. You have a responsibility to maintain your health for her sake. Surely you are a mature and responsible adult. Think about it."

I have thought about it. I resent being reminded that my dietary scruples are self-centered. I also object to insinuations that my attitudes may be childish. Comments like that are certainly worth pouting about.

But it is the accusation behind his words which particularly irritates me. If you are truly concerned, why don't you do something about it? Your actions, or failure to act, reveal either a lack of concern or a certain amount of belligerence. Which is it? We both know the correct answer is ''a certain amount of belligerence.'' There is only one thing which angers me more than having to admit to myself that I am being obstinate and that is someone *else* making an issue of it.

It is obvious why I dislike dieticians. They are annoyingly tuned in to my weakest self. In the dietician's defense, I was later informed that he had misunderstood the doctor's report and thought that I was refusing to eat, which is something I have never done. That is why he came on so strong. Those considerations aside, everything he said is still true.

Dieticians make me nervous because they have an uncanny way of uncovering the fact that I am often my own worst enemy in the battle to overcome my disabilities. If it were not dieticians, it would be someone else, anyone, who came into contact with areas of my life which I have barely begun to master.

I'm sure, when I think about it, that the temptations which faced Jesus in the wilderness were the temptations he would have the greatest difficulty resisting. I mean, if you're going to home in on a weakness, why do it half-heartedly? That wouldn't make sense to either a devil or a dietician.

Like everyone else, I suppose, I *am* often my own worst enemy. Over the years, I have cultivated many strategies which militate against my own best interests. They originate from various life experiences, but can be identified as being of two general types.

The first are those barriers I construct by setting limits to my attempts to lead a fulfilled life. In the past, I have made many assumptions about what I would be able to achieve. For example, as I mentioned earlier, the two major assumptions I made during my late teens were that I would never be able to live away from my parents' home, and that I would have to remain single. For a time these assumptions kept me from achieving those very ends because they negatively influenced my attitudes and actions in situations which could have led to those goals. They had the potential of becoming self-fulfilling prophecies.

The second barrier, related to the first but more difficult to overcome, consists of the self-centeredness, conceits, prejudices, and preoccupations which sometimes misdirect the flow of my energies. One source of these self-defeating responses is the sense that I have lost, or have never had, control over significant areas of my life. So much of what comes to me in life, I experience as being predetermined.

I did not ask to be born with CF. True, no one else can control their own genetic makeup either. Yet, as a result of having CF, I have less control than a normal person over my health and bodily functioning. Yes, there *are* things I can do to make myself as healthy as possible under the circumstances. But the disease process itself is degenerative and progresses in relatively predictable stages. In Canada, the average life expectancy of a person with CF is 24 years, although at the clinic where I now attend it is 30 years. I am now 26 years old. For me, time is running out. While no one ultimately has control over, or can prevent, their own death, it feels as if I have significantly less control.

Specific treatment for the disease is also largely predetermined. The only choice you have is to follow the treatment routine and achieve some relative degree of health, or not to follow it and suffer the consequences. Some choice.

But it *is* a choice. And it is here that self-defeating responses can gain a foothold.

Surely most people would like to experience the world and their life on their own terms. I certainly would. But so many choices which appear open to others, for me appear to be genetically preprogramed. Thus, I have often responded by rebelling against any external control, that is, by ensuring that in those areas of my life which *are* under my control, I will exercise that control. I *will!*

At one time or another, the attempt has entailed a refusal to let a specific therapy schedule or diet dictate my existence. Usually, these attempts resulted in harmful, or at least dubious, physical consequences. One might think, therefore, that I would choose to assert control of my destiny in less delicate areas of my life, like schooling and vocation. But while I try to assert control over *all* aspects of my life, it is the things which I experience as unavoidably restrictive, like therapy and diet, which are most likely to elicit my destructive, retaliatory responses.

Like a child rebelling against what he or she perceives to be an unjustly demanding parent, I petulantly assert that if I can not have things my way, I won't have them at all. I *will* have control.

The subtlety of these responses is evident in that I do not feel as though I am acting unreasonably. I have become so adept at rationalizing my responses that it is difficult for me to tell when this forms the basis of my actions. (Alcoholics, I'm told, have the same enviable ability to convince themselves that their addiction is entirely normal and reasonable.)

The issue of exercise can be, for me, almost as volatile as that of diet. A light to moderate exercise program would benefit my general health greatly, as well as build up physical resources and stamina against more serious physical set-backs. And yet I do not exercise regularly because I have managed to rationalize my decision. You see, I already spend two or more hours a day on health related activities. I could spend my entire day on them. But there is more to life than the pursuit of health. I have other things I would like to do, other goals I would like to achieve. One has to draw the line somewhere. Doesn't one? See, it's easy. I'm not being unreasonable, irresponsible or petulant. I am simply making an informed, if possibly regrettable, lifestyle decision. You're right, I am being pig-headed. There is no way a half hour of exercise each day is going to prevent me from achieving my other goals. It may even help. But it seems so much easier to rebel than make the best of a bad situation.

Rationalizing my reluctance to force-feed myself is just as easy. Although I was quite ill, it was not until I was almost two years old that doctors reached a correct diagnosis of my condition. As a result, my digestive problems were ineffectively treated during that first crucial two years. I suffered from severe cramping and diarrhea. Psychologists will tell you that it is during this period that oral traits are determined. It remains as no surprise, at least to me, that even to this day food holds no particular allure.

To be honest, I am not sure whether I believe the explanation myself. It does come in handy, however, when trying to explain to *someone else* my reasonable aversion to stuffing my face in order to gain weight. Such rationalizing is also a fine way of absolving myself of any personal responsibility for my current situation—something I am, of course, anxious to do.

The feeling of having little control over significant areas of my life is not the only source of my self-defeating actions and the rationalizing which I use to support them. Often I simply succumb to ordinary self-centeredness. At times, I am just not interested in looking beyond my own preferences especially if I think considering others will negatively affect my own concerns. Actually, having a handicap probably increases the likelihood of self-absorption. In the novel *Hand-Me-Downs* by Rhea Kohan, I found a description of a character which explains beautifully how this situation happens.

Neil, the fictitious character, was a premature baby. For many weeks, even months, his parents were afraid that he would not survive. But he lived, much to their delight. The greatest desire of Neil's parents was simply that he continue to do so. Anything that Neil got or didn't get, did or didn't do, was marvelous, just as long as he didn't die. They took the fact that he did not die as a sign of filial fondness toward them. Neil grew up thinking there was a good chance he was the Messiah.

Messiah complex aside, I relate to several elements of this description. Certainly fear of a child's death is always present for the parents of any cystic child, although they may demonstrate that fear in varying ways and degrees. My parents are no exception. I also remember coming home with my first report card and asking my mother if D's were good. She said D's were just fine for me. I had been sick a lot that year.

I am not criticizing either my parents' fear or their unconditional encouragement. I have my own fears regarding death. Furthermore, I am no doubt happier, healthier, and better adjusted now than I would be if my mother, after seeing my report card, had slapped me around a bit and said, "You better do better or else . . . ."

Perhaps all I am really saying is that having a disability does not exempt a person from many of the conceits and self-preoccupations of the general populace. I am certainly no exception.

The dietician's reminder that I need to consider my responsibilities to Jan, and her dependence on me, upsets me precisely because I would prefer not to consider those responsibilities. Extending the issue of my diet to include those with whom I live reminds me of the self-centeredness of past decisions and behavior.

In my struggle over food, it is *my* inconvenience, *my* comfort, *my* happiness, which has been the motivating factor. Refusing to make the extra effort to eat correctly may in the short run be more "convenient" for me. But when it threatens *my* health, it also threatens the happiness and stability of our home. I often forget, too, that to "inconvenience" myself by eating properly truly inconveniences Jan, because an ideal diet for me is not a balanced diet for her.

Once I shift the focus from myself to others, it becomes much more difficult to rationalize or sustain any argument that supports my old ways of functioning.

But I like the old ways. I like being the center of attention.

When I begin to consider the needs of others it feels too much as though something outside myself has again started to determine my life and I have lost control—none of which is true.

In *A Touch of Wonder*, Arthur Gordon has written that "Most of us spend our lives trying to escape from self-centeredness. Maybe that's the whole point, the whole challenge, what the whole thing is all about. Some of us succeed better than others. It seems to me that the ones who have most success are those who somehow turn self-caring into what might be called other-caring."

It strikes me that, as a life task, the "escape from self-centeredness" is also the prime religious task, with the same goal, other-caring, as its purpose. "You shall love the Lord your God with all your heart, and with all your soul, and with all your strength, and with all your mind; and your neighbor as yourself," (Lk. 10:27). Turning the focus of one's existence toward God, and God's presence in our neighbor, is the essence of a life of faith.

To turn toward God, in faith, is in some measure to turn away from the self. Faith in God implies the recognition that I myself am not the center of the universe. My raison d'etre, my reason for being, is found beyond myself in at least two ways. First, I recognize that I did not create myself, I am not responsible for my own existence. And second, I *am* responsible to someone beyond myself for the way in which I live out that existence.

The call to live my faith represents and involves decision-making and choice. Looking beyond myself to God and others does not imply relinquishing control of my life. It means, rather, accepting responsibility for redirecting the flow of my life, outward as well as inward, toward God and my neighbor as well as toward myself.

Living my faith does not mean that I am to avoid self-knowledge. Knowledge and understanding of self are requisite for truly understanding, considering, and caring for others. And the call to love our neighbors as ourselves *does* call for us to love ourselves. A mature faith is one which can incorporate both my own and my neighbor's well-being.

Nor is the call to look beyond myself necessarily a call to give up my own desires or best interests. It is a challenge to *continually re-evaluate* those interests. For example, am I really serving myself by indulging in my dietary scruples or my reluctance to exercise? I may gain a sense of control, but that same sense can be gained by following other, less potentially destructive, options.

Looking outward instead of inward also helps me overcome these self-imposed limitations. For years I assumed I would never marry. I thought it unlikely that I would ever meet someone who could look and love beyond my limitations. As a result, I entered only "safe" relationships where long term commitment or possible rejection was neither an issue nor a danger. I found, however, that when I honestly turned to another in unguarded caring and love, I was accepted in kind.

My decision to forego the security of my home environment and return to school entailed a similar outward outlook, with equally pleasing results.

In both my relationship with Jan and my return to school, I discovered that an assumed barrier crumbled when I dared to look beyond my own fears and presuppositions. In protecting myself, I also denied myself opportunities to love and be loved.

Unfortunately, the attempt to direct one's perspective outward does not come with any guarantees. Jan's decision to enter into an intentional and committed relationship was as much a risk for her as for me. As a couple we are still susceptible to rejection.

As positive as our relationship has been, for Jan and myself, our decision to marry was not met with unanimous approval. Before we announced our engagement, Jan and I spent time visiting with many of her friends as a way of introducing me to them and them to me. It was a testing of the community waters, so to speak.

After one such visit, I said to Jan, "I don't think she approves." It was nothing overt, just an intuitive hunch. My hunch proved accurate. When Jan's friend later learned of our engagement, her reaction was hostile. In ensuing conversations, it became apparent that she was presenting Jan with an either/or decision. Their relationship could remain as it had for years, or

Jan could marry me and lose a friend. Jan lost a friend.

Nor is there anything easy about looking beyond my fears, preoccupations, and my own self-centeredness. Dieticians still make me uneasy. They simply remind me that many of my driving forces remain untamed. The temptation to balk often proves stronger than the call to change. But simply recognizing the need to change may be half the battle.

The ultimate challenge

CHAPTER SIX

I went to visit Richard in the room down the hall. He's a lot sicker than I am, this time.

Besides CF, he and I have a lot in common. We are the same age. We have a similar body build, or lack thereof. We are both university students. We both dislike being in hospital, especially at the start of the school year.

I shared with Richard my frustration at having to miss school. I asked him if this hospital stay would affect his school year. He said he was not thinking about school so much anymore. Earlier in the day the doctors had told him that, this time, he would not be going home.

I asked him if the doctors had volunteered the information. No, he had insisted on knowing the prognosis. The doctors estimated that he had another two or three weeks to live. "It changes your perspective," he said.

The social worker who had come to the floor to talk to me walked by the door. It was an excuse to end the conversation. I needed time and space to think.

Several days later, I returned to Richard's room. He was painting a picture of a motorcycle, and doing a fine job for someone who had never painted. He said it was something he had always wanted to try. The nurses obliged him and provided the materials. I asked him if he would like me to drop by daily.

He said thanks, but no. He wanted to spend his remaining time and energy with his family.

Richard could afford to forego many of the games the rest of us play. *I* was the one who needed to talk. *I* was the one who needed reassurance. He tried to give it to me before I left. I was not to let his death discourage me. All that was important, he said, was that one lead a good life. Have a good life.

I left his room to return to my own and face again those questions of which I weary, those fears I cannot seem to escape.

I have had to face death many times, even from before my first conscious remembrances. Most of the experiences, except the earliest, remain clearly in mind as little vignettes, images which evoke a persistent question or possess a particular, strong, emotional undertone. I share them without interpretation. They stand simply as they are. None is more right or adequate than another. Ultimately, they are all, individually and as a whole, inadequate. They remain small glimpses of the many ways I have experienced the ultimate challenge to meaning.

★ ★ ★ ★ ★

An incident my mother shared with me.

Once, when I was about three years old, I was playing with the neighborhood children. One young girl told me that I was going to die because I had CF. I became upset and ran home crying. I asked mother, "What happens when you die?"
She hesitated and then replied, "You will go to heaven."

I had been desperately wanting a cowboy hat. I asked, "Do they have cowboy hats in heaven?" Mom said she thought they probably did. Quite pleased by this answer, I went back out to play.

★ ★ ★ ★ ★

A recurrent dream.

I am standing on a large, empty, white desert. I begin to see tiny black spots. They keep growing, getting larger and larger, coming nearer and nearer. They start to look like huge black boulders, but they keep growing and are all around me. They are just about to crush or totally envelop me, when I wake up, terrified.

★ ★ ★ ★ ★

Age eighteen, in hospital.

It is 3 a.m. I lie wide awake in my darkened room. The soft light washing in from the corridor seems strangely distant. Even more distant are the voices, the talking and laughter of the doctors and nurses down the hall.

My father, who has remained by my bedside, walks to the doorway, peers out, and lifts a finger to his lips. The voices become muted and die away.

My body burns with fever. There is fear. Then abruptly, certainty. I will *not* die. I *refuse* to die. I *will* live. I sense the presence of God, and God's acceptance of me. There is peace . . . and finally sleep.

★ ★ ★ ★ ★

At seminary.

Jan and I are newly married. How does my shortened life expectancy fit into our new life together? The thought of separation by death in only a few years is too painful to contemplate.

New relationships, new contexts, require new perspectives. As an escape, I decide to take the intellectual approach, to write a theology of death. I must prepare a biblical survey of attitudes toward death. Include both Old and New Testaments. I must relate the findings to the way we do ethics, in particular, medical ethics.

Sitting with a professor, I share the outline for my theology. The professor remains quiet throughout. When I am finished, he says simply, "Writing your theology of death may be a worthwhile task, but I wonder . . . when you are finished, will you really have found what you are looking for?"

★ ★ ★ ★ ★

Seminary ethics class, case study #3.

The text poses the problem: "I don't want to tell my sister that it's all right for her to die. But if I really love Sara, maybe that is what I have to say."

Mike S. Am I case study #4?

Late in the evening. The seminary lounge is empty. Its many windows look out, unseeing. The smooth glass panes reflect the light from within, and hide the night. I guide the vacuum as it scrounges across the floor. It takes in what crumbs can be found.

It seems as though I've been looking for answers for such a long time. I'm tired, just so tired, and so alone. I think it is difficult for most people to understand the burden placed on the dying person. Death is the last enemy, the thing to fight, the thing to overcome. The reaper's apparition must be avoided at all cost. But one can only fight so long. Exhaustion comes. The enemy proves stronger.

But I haven't given up. I haven't quit. It is okay to die. Can't

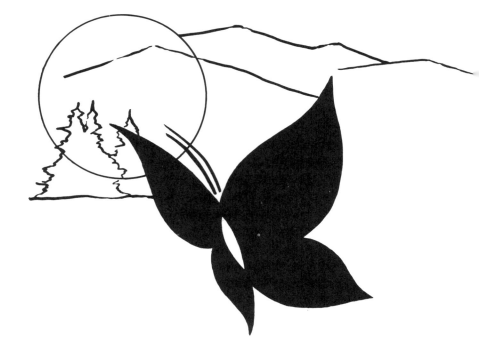

they see? Can't *I* see?

It is okay to die. Can I convince myself?

An overstuffed chair, arms open, accepts my body and my tears.

★ ★ ★ ★ ★

Danny. He and I could have been brothers. We were both students, he and I. Both quiet. We met in the hospital, several times. It's strange how the same group of people end up being hospitalized at the same time, time after time.

Danny died a week or so ago. I just found out. I was out of town that week. I missed the funeral. Now, as I lie back on the bed, tears in my eyes, I wonder who I mourn. Is it he or is it I?

★ ★ ★ ★ ★

Jennifer. Blond hair, blue eyes, a genuine beauty. Jennifer, a quiet young woman, possessed of a maturity and poise beyond her fourteen years.

Jennifer, with an accepting way and simple grace, you lift up those who share in your life.

The subway bursts out from its subterranean passageway, and continues on into the gloom of the day. Dark clouds and raindrops. Oh Jennifer, must you too die? An all too brief visit to your hospital bed tells me it must be so. Raindrops on the subway window wind their way from top to bottom, and obscure the world rushing past.

The call came a day later. Jennifer, with family by her side, had died, only hours after I saw her last.

Sitting in the last row of chairs, in a chapel overflowing, I mark the tears of those around me, and wish that I too, could find such release. I *want* to cry! I'm exhausted, empty, detached. Why can't I cry? A rain of tears would wash and soothe the ache, would fill the void, would fill my well. Has my spring run dry? Is there nothing left?

★ ★ ★ ★ ★

Hospital room.

Being on a small ward in a children's hospital has its
drawbacks.✶ There are only two private rooms reserved for the
older patients and for the dying. This time I qualify only as an
older patient. But what about next time?

Richard lay here, where I do now. Richard looked out this
same window, to the world beyond. Richard, and Robby,
Jennifer, and countless others too. All gone.

It's unnerving to be brought back, again and again, to stand
upon the same gallows and confront the same executioner. And
each time never knowing. Do I receive another pardon, or not?

This time, I am simply an older patient. What about
next time?

★Because the CF clinic was originally established for children—at that time,
few survived long enough to become adults—older patients still return to the
children's hospital for treatment.

In
this
life

CHAPTER SEVEN

For the past week, I have been trying to put on paper my thoughts and feelings about suffering and death. I haven't been doing very well. Somewhere in the middle of the second or third sentence, I find myself unable to continue. Each time it happens, I turn a page and try a new approach. But again, after only a few sentences I can go no further.

The problem is not that I am reluctant to think or talk about death. On the contrary, I sometimes worry that I think about death too much. And people tell me that they find me quite willing to talk about death.

The problem lies in trying to distill the vastness of the experience of death into a few pages. An encounter with death is really an encounter with the whole of life. Trying to write a few pages on the significance of death is as impossible a task as condensing the significance of life to a few pages.

I respond to death on all the levels on which I experience life. Sometimes my encounter with death has occurred on an undifferentiated level, as a primal experience. At these times, all I can form are the vaguest impressions; mere insinuations of emotional stirrings, and the tiniest hints of conceptual content.

To borrow a phrase from Joseph Conrad, on this level, I experience death as an "impalpable greyness." It is an experience which defies description, the only sure thing being a sense of uneasiness.

In stark contrast, I have often tried to intellectualize the encounter with death. I have studied death as a biological phenomenon and have asked, what, biologically speaking, constitutes death. Is it lack of respiration, lack of pulse, or a flat EEG indicating brain death? Is it some combination of these? Or is death better defined from a relational perspective which includes medical criteria? Has death occurred when a person is no longer able to form meaningful relationships; for example, someone in an irreversible coma? Continuing the process, I have taken biological considerations, medical definitions of death, and have asked in what ways these apply to our practice of medical ethics.

As a religious studies student, I have been eager to find a theological balm for the pain of death. Writing my theology of death was part of that process. I did biblical surveys, book studies, word studies. I can think of a myriad other ways of studying death from a religious perspective, enough to preoccupy a lifetime.

But I think it is my emotional responses which embody my most profound experience of death. An honest encounter with death is a powerful emotional experience. I have felt fear, because death remains the great unknown. At other times, I have felt the profound sadness that comes at the prospect of ending relationships. It is the sorrow of saying final good-byes. Of coming to endings. As a friend commented to his family: "You're just losing me. I'm losing everything."

And, irrational as it may be, I am usually left with a sense of guilt. I suppose most people experience guilt upon the death of someone they love. How many times have people lamented, "If only . . . ." For myself, it has been difficult to discard the thought that in death I will be disappointing those people I care about most. My own feelings of guilt have found the same expression. "If only . . . . If only I had done more therapy, eaten more, exercised more, done anything *more*!"

Such feelings of guilt lead to anger. "We *did* do the best we could to ensure mother's health! And she *still* died!" "I *was* watching the kids! But you can't be by their sides every minute!''

Again, for myself; ''I *did* try my best! I just wasn't strong enough!''

Even without such feelings of guilt, I have been angry. Suffering and death don't play fair. Death seldom seems just, especially if it strikes at an early age. As a result, I have felt persecuted and unjustly maligned, by life and by God. And at times, I have allowed such feelings to dictate my approach to life.

These responses may all be valid. But they cannot, of themselves, give the experience of death any creative value and meaning.

Richard died a week after I was released from hospital. Later, speaking to the hospital chaplain, I learned that Richard had given those who participated in his dying a gift. Richard's openness and honesty in sharing his feelings toward death had been a gift to his family, his friends, even to the hospital staff, especially to the nurses who were responsible for his care during the final weeks. Richard faced death with an integrity that transformed the dreaded event of losing a child, a brother, and a friend, into a positive—if painful—opportunity for growth.

I don't know if Richard was a religious person in the traditional sense. I do believe, however, that if Richard and his family were at all able to cope with his death, it was because, somehow, they recognized death as being part of life. Somehow, they were able to integrate suffering and death into their concept of life and life's source of meaning, whether or not they called it God.

Because death is as vast as life itself, and because it will ultimately absorb all my life's meanings, death needs to be approached from a perspective which grants ultimate meaning to my life. For me, this ultimate source of meaning is God. Thus a constructive encounter with death depends on relating my experience of death to my experience of God.

In my own life, I have attempted that integration at many different moments and in many different contexts. The questions I asked of God when I first realized that I would have to live with a serious handicap were not much different from those I have asked while staring at the unmasked face of death. Similarly, the emotions I experienced in trying to integrate suffering and disability into the meaning I assigned life are the same emotions I have felt when I confronted death. Suffering and death ask many of the same questions about God.

It is on an emotional level, it is in anger, that I have most often asked, "Why?" Why is there suffering, why death? Why me? Why is this happening to me? What have I done to deserve this?

As such, the cry, "Why me!", is much less a question begging an answer, than it is an exclamation, a note of anguish, begging for sympathy and understanding.

But more often than not, the plea, "God, why me?" is *treated* as a genuine question. In my experience, the common "answers" give as much pain and alienation as suffering and death itself.

I once attended a funeral for a very young child. At one point during the service, members of the congregation were invited to respond to the parents. One person stood and said that the parents could take heart. God had had a special purpose for their child on earth. But now God wanted, or needed, the child back. God had a purpose in mind, and had called the child home.

The comments were meant to console and comfort. They did not have that effect. On the contrary, they created anguish and anger. To a grieving person, the suggestion that his or her loss occurred as an act of God's will is almost unbearable.

Earlier in my own experience, during the period when I asked many "Why me?" questions of God, I entertained many possible solutions in my head. The idea that God had willed me having CF was one of them. The belief made me angry. God, whom I'd always been told was a loving God, seemed anything but loving. I felt as though I had been betrayed. I was not a morally perfect person, but I had never done anything to merit such punishment. And if my having CF was not punishment, but perhaps meant to be a learning experience, I decided I would rather remain unenlightened.

No matter how I cut it, any attempt to rationalize my suffering as being a part of God's *will,* left me hurt, angry, and alienated. I could not love a God who, seemingly, would not love me, or would only love me while hurting me.

Fortunately, anger takes energy—something I did not have in excess. The anger lessened. Also, my desire was to be close to God. As a result of those two factors, I called a moratorium on "Why me?" questions. They weren't helping, and they sure seemed to hurt.

I was still left with the question "Why?" in general. Why does God allow suffering and death to happen, not just to me, but to anyone?

It occurred to me that not only did I not want that answer, I didn't want *any* answer. I was not looking for a *reason* to bear my suffering. I was looking for *compassion.* No answer, no reason, I realized, would relieve the pain and hurt resulting from my lost health and wholeness. I did not want an explanation, but rather, comfort and consolation. I wanted God and those around me to know how much I hurt. I wanted to be loved and held. I wanted something to fill the emptiness my loss left within me. No answer could accomplish such a feat.

At its most profound level, the cry "Why!" might not require an answer, but I believe it does plead for a response. And there is a response.

I believe God has provided the response. In the alienation, suffering, and death of Christ, I witness a God who has shared in all the pain of human experience. Christ's prayer in Gethsemane, ". . . if it be possible, let this cup pass from me" (Matt. 26:39), strikes me as a powerful symbol of God's identification with, and participation in, the human experience, through the suffering of Christ.

The question, then, is no longer, "Why does God allow suffering?", but, "How does God relate to us in our suffering?" The response of God, symbolized in the life and death of Christ, is one of compassion. Compassion means, literally, "to suffer with."

At the university, I participated in a tutorial session for a comparative religions course. We were discussing the nature and origins of evil, as well as theological responses to the question.

At one point, I suggested that the relation of God to human suffering and death was not one of cause-and-effect. God does not necessarily *will* or *cause* suffering and death. Rather, God *participates* in our suffering.

The tutorial leader acknowledged that the concept of a suffering God was a response to the problem of evil, a concept that had been put forward at different times by various people. "But," he asked, "doesn't the idea of deity transcend human experience? After all, God is not human. Is it really appropriate to speak of a God who suffers? Can God really suffer?"

If I were asked the same question today, I would say, "Yes, God suffers. In the manner and extent to which it is appropriate to say that God *loves* it is appropriate to say that God *suffers.*" Suffering is an integral part of loving. Only those who really love can really suffer.

The person who has lost a friend, the husband or wife who has lost a spouse, the parents who have lost a child, suffer *because* of their identification and participation in the life of the other, through love.

Only if you are willing to say that God does not truly love can you say that God does not suffer. But the God to whom I respond in faith is a loving God and therefore also a compassionate, sympathetic, suffering God.

I don't believe this as an intellectual, theological balm for the pain of suffering and death. The pain remains. So too may the anger. The pain remains because ending a lifetime of relationships is a painful process. Anger may remain because suffering and death never feel particularly just. Suffering and death may be the result of our society's own moral guilt: through war, systemic and social violence, human irresponsibility. Or it may be the result of natural disaster, or the result of disease and the afflictions that plague all living organisms.

But my anger can now be focused more appropriately on the situation, rather than on God.

Others, may still find cause to be angry with God. The world is not perfect. Couldn't God have made a perfect world in which there would have been no suffering and death? For myself, I do not know why the world is not perfect, and I don't know if God could have created a perfect world. Some would argue, and I tend to agree, that an imperfect world is the price of human freedom.

But such questions seem to me to be of doubtful value. Some aspects of life will remain forever unanswerable. More helpful, to my mind, is to recognize God's participation in, and suffering with, the world God *did* create.

I say this not because I fear God will punish my anger. God is surely able to understand and accept my anger. I am not likely to hurt God's feelings. But what I will more likely hurt, at the very time I need it most, is my own sense of nearness to and communion with God.

If instead, I direct my anger at the "injustice" of the circumstances which result in my suffering, I can offer up my feelings to God in the assurance that God understands and shares in them. I may even discover God's ability to transform my feelings, and me.

When I am faced with the reality of suffering and death, I do not need an explanation of why such things must be so. What I need is the strength and courage to make the best of my situation. I need the power to transform it into an opportunity for growth. In the process I may be transformed myself.

I receive the power and courage to face my suffering and tap its creative energy, through the love, support, and encouragement of the community which sustains me. And ultimately, the power of the community to sustain me has its source in the compassionate love of God.

Here, the resurrection remains a profound reminder of the transforming power of God, on all levels of life experience. The resurrection is the power of God to bring us to new life, in this life. God is able to transform our experience of the present. The resurrection is also the power of God to bring us to new life in a relationship which goes beyond death.

I find reassurance in the words of Paul:
"I am sure that neither death, nor life, nor angels, nor principalities, nor things present, nor things to come, nor powers, nor height, nor depth, nor anything else in all creation, will be able to separate us from the love of God in Christ Jesus our Lord" (Rom. 8:38).

Life
in the
park

CHAPTER EIGHT

Life goes on. It always does. And though my September
hospital admission is eighteen months distant, the joys and trials
of life are ever present.

There is a park a short walk from our apartment. For Jan and
me the park is one of our joys. On a spring morning, it is a
vibrant place. Everything is green and fresh. The sun shines
brightly through the trees, casting shadows and creating pools of
light and dark upon the sweet smelling grass. We pause by a
lilac bush, faces amongst the blossoms. Can anything match
such fragrance? Nearby, beneath the many pine trees clustered
about, last year's needles form a rusty brown carpet, and the
smell of pine mingles with the scents of the morning air.
Above, dozens of pine cones hang tenuously from the
lofty boughs.

The inhabitants of the park like it here too. The black squir-
rels, dashing busily from tree to tree, stop and cast a glance our
way. Visitors to their sanctuary are welcome. On a large rock
warmed by the sun, a robin sits and marks our progress. A
rustling in the bushes draws our attention. A baby bird cries
impatiently as its mother gathers seeds in her beak for the
hungry youngster. Everywhere there is bird song and cry. Surely it must be a challenge to see who has the loudest voice.

Suddenly, the park truncates itself. We have reached the

bluffs, cliffs which fall two hundred feet or more to the lake shore. Etched upon their face is evidence of an age no human ever saw. Layered, one on top of the other, glaciers have left deposits, signatures of their passing. Made of durable stuff, the cliffs remain, home to hundreds of swallows.

Lapping at the foot of the bluffs, the lake too remains. Stretching out to the horizon, sky and water meet, and trade shades of blue. The lake has shades to spare. Dark, cool blue for the depths. Bright aqua for the shallows. And closer by the beach, the sand, unsettled, creates a new hue. In the sunlight, the water sparkles, almost blinding, under our gaze. The air, cool and fresh, tickles and teases our lungs, which can't drink

their fill.

On a spring morning such as this, the park is a revitalizing place. Here, with an oak tree for support, we can sit and bask in the newness of life. It's as if the life around us has forgotten the winter. Too busy to care, if they remember at all, the birds attend and teach their newborn. The trees! Surely the trees must remember. But then, they've seen many more winters, and springs, than we. They can afford to be unimpressed.

I remember the winter, cold and barren. In the midst of its darkness this new life seemed far away. It *was* too far . . . for Danny and Jennifer. Then again, they probably found spring long before I did.

Yes. It was a long, hard winter. But it hasn't been just the winter. The last year and a half has been numbing. Two weeks after my first admission in September eighteen months ago, I caught a cold and found myself back in the hospital. And then again, in March. I was admitted in August, and again for most of December and early January. In the process, I have dropped from four courses at the university, to three, and now to two. During the same time, six friends and acquaintances with CF have died. First there was Richard, then Robby, Karen and Sally, Danny and Jennifer. On top of all this life's other concerns—a difficult job situation for Jan, too many bills, too little money—continue to weigh heavily. In the face of such loss and stress, life seems to get more difficult to live by the day. There are times when life seems devoid of meaning and hope. Perhaps the very elderly also know this feeling.

But living seems to be what I am called to do. It's what we are all called to do, isn't it? Life is nothing if it is not lived fully, in an appreciative sort of way, with meaning and hope.

And I have hope. It is not an unrealistic fantasy about what might some day happen or be possible. I don't expect any miracle cures. On the contrary, my hope is grounded in the present. My hope is grounded in my present physical condition, in my present relationships with Jan, family, friends and church community—in short, in my present realities, and in the chance that I can change my perceptions of that reality, if only I would listen to the voice of God calling in my night.

Some might think such a hope too abstract. In fact, there are some very concrete ways I can work toward such a change of perspective.

To begin, I can work to overcome the temptation to dwell on the "if only's." *If only* I had done this, *if only* I had done that. If only Jan and I could have more time together. Once something has happened, I cannot turn back the clock and rewrite history. I cannot bring to life someone who has died. I cannot undo the damage done to my lungs years earlier when I did only minimal therapy. Certain things cannot be changed.

The question, "Why?" can be as misleading as the lament, "If only." To unceasingly ask why something had to happen is to dwell on a past I no longer control and cannot change.

I am not suggesting by this that we give up our search for responsibility. To be sure, if I know the brakes on my car don't work, but I drive anyway and kill someone, I need to be held accountable. Similarly, if I enter a hospital and my condition worsens through negligence on the part of medical staff, or in the administering of treatment, I may rightly ask "why" such a thing had to happen. In such a case, I ask the question, not wishing that I could rewrite history, but in the hope of influencing the future, in the hope of preventing a similar occurrence from happening again.

But if after I have done all I can do to prevent a situation from reoccurring, I *still* continually ask why it had to happen, I have fallen into the trap of going through life facing backwards.

By focusing on what *is* possible for me to do and achieve, I have a better chance of changing my perception of the present. Instead of asking, "Why?" I can ask, "Now that this has happened, what can I do about it?"

Under the stress of trying to cope with six deaths in so short a time, I easily become fatalistic and despair of finding meaning in life. Richard was aware of that possibility. Richard knew that I might allow his death to scare me to the point where I would be afraid to go on living. Thus his final words of exhortation and counsel: "I don't want you to let my death get you down. All that is important is that one lead a good life. Have a good life."

It would be difficult to find reasons and ways to continue living, to have a good life, if I were to try to live facing backward; if I continually tried to rewrite history in my head, so that Richard would not have died. I believe that Richard, being honest, would not have approved of the attempt.

If I truly desire to find meaning and live with hope, I must recognize that, yes, I have lost six peers in the last year and a half, and yes, it hurts. It would be unnatural if I weren't depressed for a time. But eventually, I need to realize that all my wishing cannot bring any one of them back.

More helpful than dwelling on what cannot be, is looking ahead. Now that this has happened, what am I going to do about it? Will I let the pain destroy my appreciation of life, my appreciation for Jan, my family, the chance to go to school and learn? How can I best regain my appreciation and desire for life?

I once faced the same questions in less traumatic situations. Yes, I had to spend two months of the school year in the hospital. It *does* represent a loss. Understandably, I got angry. But once it has happened, should I live in the past and simply give up, or can I drop a course, rearrange my schedule, and find other ways to continue?

I should acknowledge here that there is another reason why I might find it difficult to shift my perspective from the past to the present and the future. After all the "If only's" and "Why's," I recognize that at times, consciously or otherwise, I perpetuate my own ill-feelings.

In fact, I sometimes take a perverse pleasure in wallowing in my own misfortune and misery. I prolong my anger or pain, because I enjoy the consolation of others, and especially, myself. I *like* to feel sorry for myself. No one lends me sympathy quite as well as I do.

Even better, I can excuse myself for feeling miserable by consoling myself that I have just cause for feeling the way I do.

There is another way I become my own worst enemy. After a setback such as frequent hospitalization, or trauma of witnessing several deaths, I am likely to set a whole new set of arbitrary and artificial limits on what I can expect or attempt to achieve.

The danger lies in the possibility that such limits will become self-fulfilling prophecies.

Overcoming self-pity and self-constructed barriers is not easy. But just recognizing that to some extent I create my own problems will probably help.

Deciding that I will look for new options, new ways to give my life hope and meaning, does not mean that such decisions or changes will be easy or painless.

But now, the third thing I may recognize is that I am *not* alone in my pain and frustration. No one is self-sustaining— physically, emotionally, or spiritually. No one can get through life on their own steam. But together, Jan and I, with the support of our community, find the strength and desire to continue.

And yet it becomes difficult to explain the contradictions to which I fall prey. For example, if asked, I would assert my reliance upon God for the upkeep and maintenance of my faith relationship with God. I would confess that, when left to my own devices, I quickly become skeptical both of the world in which I live and the life I lead. I would confess how easily I lose my appreciation for life and those around me. I would affirm that it is God who imparts an appreciation for life and those around me; it is God, who strengthens me in the battle against skepticism, *through* the caring of those who share in my life. Although on occasion I experience the nearness and caring of God in a more immanent way, I recognize that most often, God lifts and sustains me, spiritually *through other people.*

After admitting all that, I'm appalled to realize how often I still assume that I should be emotionally, even physically, self-sustaining.

When I am depressed, I find it difficult to express to others my feelings and frustrations, and to seek their support. I believe that I should have the inner resources to overcome my problems without the aid of others. In my head I often say, ''I should be able to work this out myself.''

The fact that I am not physically self-sustaining is just as hard to acknowledge, though perhaps less so for me than a healthy person. Yet, I often presume that if I mix therapy, diet, exercise and rest, in proper proportion, I can, or should be able to, guarantee my own health. The reality is far more complex.

My body, my life, is such a delicate thing, dependent upon so many other factors outside myself. The food I eat is grown by farmers. The medicine I take is manufactured by chemists working for large companies. My daily routine requires the aid of Jan, and sometimes others. And there is the ultimate dependency of life itself on the mystery which sustains and grants self-awareness and intelligence to a fragile mass of organic matter.

The belief that I could somehow be emotionally or physically self-sustaining becomes even more suspect when I admit that such categories of self are somewhat artificial. My experience of God and my physical and emotional health, are not separate but interrelated. Each functions to the detriment or benefit of the other. I depend on others for the well-being of my "parts." Because my "parts" are all interrelated and interfunctioning, I am dependent upon others for the well-being of my whole being.

The realization that I am not alone, then, includes the recognition that I am not self-sustaining, but am a person sharing dependencies common to all persons.

Sometimes I refuse to turn to others in my search for hope and meaning, because I presume that I am *experientially* alone. No one else has experienced what *I* have. No one has experienced exactly my pain. How can *you* who have not lived through what I have lived through, help *me* find meaning in my experience?

It is true. I am a unique person with unique life experiences, which have brought me at one time joy, gladness, and laughter; and at another, pain, fear, and alienation. But in my calmer moments, I recognize too, the mutuality of all such life experience. I may not hurt for the specific reason someone else hurts, but the questions and longings such pain arouses are similar. You may not have as limited a life expectancy as I do, but you too will die sometime. I may not be made glad by the same things as you, but the hope for, and the experience of, a fulfilled life are common to both of us.

Life gains meaning and hope as I recognize that all people are interdependent. I can therefore seek strength and nurture in the sharing of our common experience.

As I continue to search, the fourth and perhaps the most important thing I can remember is that meaning and hope are not objective, external things which can impose themselves upon my life. My search for meaning is, rather, an attempt to fit myself into the world around me in a meaningful way. My search for meaning, then, is really a search for identity.

I realize now that my search for self-worth and definition is most often derailed in one of two directions. Sometimes I have restricted my search for value and meaning to something within myself. At other times, I have concentrated on something external.

During those times when I seek meaning externally, I am prone to identify myself with "what I do." The problem arises when I am less able to do "what I do," when, for example, I have to drop courses.

Besides the havoc this creates with my own sense of self, such an identification between my identity and role has grave social implications. Such an identification reduces me to a social role or function, to a "means" rather than an "end," valued and valuable in myself. This is how society often assigns value, especially to disabled and aged persons. Once I am no longer able to perform my assigned role in society, I am of less worth and can be discarded.

As a corrective, I can remember that my value, my identity, my meaning, is not exclusively external to myself. I am of worth, not because of what I do or produce, but because I *am.* Life, my life, has an inherent value.

But at the other end of the continuum, I run into trouble when I come to think that my value and meaning are "self" created and internally sustained. This extreme denies the reality that society *does* assign value. I am not an island. I need to recognize the fact, and to find some way to integrate society's label with what I know to be true of myself.

Furthermore, if I focus on myself, I easily become too self-concerned. Yes, I have inherent worth and dignity as a human being. But I may begin to believe that every minor upset or humiliation I suffer poses a genuine threat to my dignity and

identity. Soon, almost anything can become a denigration of
self. Although I detest having to collect the occasional stool
specimen, the distasteful duty hardly represents a serious
challenge to my self-worth or identity. It is possible to take
myself *too* seriously. There are simply many situations in which
I am best served by a sense of perspective and a sense
of humor.

Finally, at this extreme, I discover that I am impotent to
create my own meaning and value in any transcendent sense. To
find meanihg for my life as a whole, and to live with hope, I
must ultimately look beyond myself. I need an identity which
can grant meaning, not just to my present situation, but to my
entire life story—past, present, and future.

The only identity which can grant such meaning is discovered
through my relationships with family, community, and God.

The love and acceptance I receive from Jan, family, and
significant others, is not conditional on my success or failure in
school or job. It is not conditional on my ability to cope
emotionally, on whether I'm angry and depressed, or relaxed
and accepting. It is a love which grants meaning and hope as
together, we lift one another up to our fullest potential as
persons in communion with creation and the Creator.

Such relationships are an expression of the ultimate love relationship. I discover meaning and hope in my identity as a child
of God. As in my other love relationships, meaning and hope
are here both external and indwelling. God, alone, has the
power to give ultimate meaning. Thus, meaning is found externally. My life gains meaning, not primarily through what I do
or produce, but through God. Therefore, meaning is also
indwelling because as a child of God, as a creature loved by my
Creator, my life gains an inherent worth and value.

Because of this, I can live fully and with hope.

I can live with *hope* because by orienting my life toward God
and others through faith, I allow God to fill my life with meaning it would not otherwise have. I can live *fully* because with
the hope of meaning, comes the strength and assurance to
sample whatever life has to offer.

With the hope of meaning, comes the ability to accept both

the joy and sadness which *is* life. There is joy in the living, in laughter and tears, in the excitement, delight, and anticipation of life unfolding in its fullness and in faithfulness to God and humanity. There is sadness that even a life so lived, leaves things undone, places unseen, and the pain of good-byes.

And yet, maybe a life lived fully, a life lived in faith, with hope, with others, is all that God expects. Such a life has done all there is to do, seen all there is to see, experienced all that any life has ever known or felt . . . .

Joyfully, life in the park has begun anew. It is spring.

Study Guide

FOR USE BY THE LEADERS OF GROUPS
by Jim Taylor

This study guide has been developed on the assumption that the leader has had some previous experience in leading groups. For this reason, detailed lesson plans have not been given; the plans include only suggested references within the book, and suggested questions for discussion.

Even so, a few words need to be said about adult learning patterns, and about the leader's role.

How adults learn

It's often assumed that adults learn best in a lecture or classroom format. There they can learn facts, store information, and apply it on their own. But adults don't learn that way—or at least, don't learn very well that way.

When children learn, everything is new. And they use almost everything as fast as they absorb it.

Adolescents are not yet ready to use what they're learning. They have no choice but to store information.

Adults are more selective in their learning. They learn by associating new information with what they already know or do. They learn only what they can integrate with their present lives or their plans for the future.

That pattern of learning by association has implications for the shape of study groups.

First of all, it means that adults must have opportunity to make those associations. Lecture input, by itself, is not enough. Adults will learn better if they have opportunity for discussion, in relatively small, confidential groups, where they can relate their own experiences and make connections with the new information that has been presented.

Secondly, many adults feel threatened by new learnings. If they have to integrate those learnings into their existing lives, their new understandings may upset some previous understandings. Therefore, they learn best in a non-threatening environment, where each person's experiences and opinions are valued, not judged.

The leader's role

To help these adults learn, the leader must set the example.

That means, firstly, providing a non-threatening environment. People need to be welcomed, not abandoned to their fate. Chairs can be set up in a circle or semi-circle, so that participants can see something other than the backs of other people's heads.

The opening of any group meeting is a critical time. People need to be set at ease. Sometimes this can be done by singing songs. One leader manages it with a kind of stand-up comic routine about his diet. Some use get-acquainted games or activities. Providing coffee or dessert often works well. Brainstorming sessions can involve people without risk or ridicule. Whatever method you use, remember that every group, as it is formed, will need some time to get at ease with its members—including any small groups that people go to for discussion.

Setting an example is particularly important during a time of input, if there is to be a lecture or presentation of information. If the speaker hides behind abstract principles or generalities, or refers only to other people's experiences, the participants will follow the speaker's lead. And they will never manage to associate the message with their own lives. For that reason, it's essential that those leading a study program on this book read the book thoroughly, identify ways in which this story impacts their own lives, and be willing to share that impact with others.

Study themes

Five study themes have been developed. You may tackle any or all of them, in any order.

While the program outline assumes that one theme will be handled in each session, some groups may want to examine Michael Schwartzentruber's story in greater depth, and consider one or more of the questions it raises for them over a longer period.

Session formats

We suggest a four part process:

1. A time of gathering and getting at ease with each other. This could include a period of opening worship.

2. A time for setting an example. The leader offers some input for participants, suggesting avenues of thought and reflection, and sharing personal reactions and experiences. The leader may well have additional knowledge or information to contribute, including biblical insights. (To assist leaders of large or small groups, each session includes a selection of sentences from relevant portions of the story. In some cases, wordings have been edited slightly from the book text, for brevity. The numbers identify the chapter and/or page in the book where the sentences appear.)

3. A time for private discussions, in groups of 5-8 people. This is the time when that learning by association can take place. (Each session includes suggested questions for discussion.)

4. A time of sharing, when small groups gather together again to let others share their insights and discoveries. The sharing may conclude with a closing worship or period of prayer.

SESSION ONE: SUFFERING

Purpose of session

To seek some meaning for the existence of suffering in our lives.

References

I have yet to find a satisfactory answer to the question, "Why me?" What if God had said, "Yes Mike, there is a reason . . ." Would it have really helped me to be less angry, less hurt, less broken? *(Ch. 2, 21)*

Maybe they could understand the reasoning . . . but I wonder if knowing or even agreeing helped to heal the hurt, helped to fill the sense of loss. And what if they, family and friends, did NOT agree with the decision? *(22)*

"Why me?" is less a question than an exclamation. But often it is treated as a genuine question. In my experience, the common answers give as much pain as do the suffering and death. *(Ch. 6, 62)*

Telling someone whose house has just burned down that they should be glad no one was killed may be a true statement, but it appears to minimize their loss. I need someone to recognize and share my pain and my loss. My ability to be thankful will return . . . . *(Ch. 3, 30-31)*

The cry, "God, why me?" echoes in the empty stillness of my soul. Slowly, I realize that an explanation is not what I want. I want to be comforted, consoled, I want to be loved, held. *(Ch. 1, 22)*

When I am faced with suffering and death, I do not need an explanation . . . I need the strength and courage to make the best of my situation. *(Ch. 6, 65)*

I am not alone in pain and frustration. *(Ch. 8, 72)*

When I am depressed, I find it difficult to express to others my feelings and frustrations, and to seek their support. *(72)*

It has been during these times of crisis that recognition and acceptance of my identity as a person has come. *(Ch. 2, 24)*

The question, then, is no longer, "Why does God allow suffering?" but, "How does God relate to us in our suffering?"

(Ch. 6, 63) Does God suffer? If God loves us, God suffers with us. Suffering is an integral part of loving. *(64)*

If I continually ask why something had to happen, I condemn myself to going through life facing backwards. *(Ch. 8, 70)* Looking ahead is more helpful. Now that this has happened, what am I going to do about it?'' *(70)*

Suggested questions for discussion
1. Have you ever demanded, ''Why me?'' In what situation?
2. How can a good God allow sin, evil, and suffering?
3. Is life just a lottery, in which things happen by chance? Or is there some kind of cause-and-effect relationship behind things, some purpose and meaning and intention?
4. What does God expect from us, when we do encounter suffering?

SESSION TWO: DISABILITIES

Purpose of session
To consider the kinds of disabilities that people experience, and to see how those disabilities can affect our lives.

References
For a disabled person, questions of self image arise not only during times of crisis. *(Ch. 3, 26)*

In a fast paced society, first impressions carry a lot of weight. As a result, most of us like to put our best foot forward. But for many people with a disability, "putting your best foot forward" is simply not possible, using society's concept of "best foot." Many simply don't have the luxury of concealing their "shortcomings" until they feel comfortable in a relationship. *(26)*

I discovered an acceptance and friendship which was not hampered but enhanced as we shared my handicap. My weakness, my dependence, became an unexpected asset. *(28)*

My body, my life, is such a delicate thing, dependent on so many other factors outside myself. *(Ch. 8, 73)*

Barriers crumbled when I dared look beyond my own fears. In protecting myself, I am also denying myself opportunities to love and be loved. *(Ch. 5, 51)*

Acceptance of who I am begins on those rare occasions when I remember that I am first and foremost a creature loved by my Creator. My sense of who I am depends on my relationship to God. I am of infinite worth, no matter what my personal limitations. *(Ch. 3, 31)*

The love and acceptance I receive from Jan, family, and others, is not conditional on my success or failure in school or job . . . . Such relationships are an expression of the ultimate love relationship. *(Ch. 8, 75)*

Suggested questions for discussion
1. What kinds of disabilities are you familiar with? Cystic Fibrosis might be considered an invisible disability. What other invisible disabilities are there?
2. Which is more of a handicap—a disability itself, or people's

attitudes towards that disability? How about the attitudes of the person who has the disability?

3. Does accepting something mean giving up?

4. How does our society (church, community) deal with disability in its midst?

SESSION THREE: LIMITATIONS

Purpose of session
To examine the ways in which we become our own worst enemies, and to find ways to change that.

References
The desire to put my best foot forward represents only half my dilemma. The other half is my wish that it be Robert Redford's foot. *(Ch. 3, 29)*
The tensions and anxieties I experience in new relationships are minor compared to those I create for myself. *(29)*
Few people are satisfied with who they are. *(29)*
By equating myself with what I do or produce, I create most of my own problems and tensions. If I am less able to be a student, then I am somehow less of a person. *(31)*
Acceptance of who I am begins on those rare occasions when I remember that I am first and foremost a creature loved by my Creator. My sense of who I am depends on my relationship to God. I am of infinite worth, no matter what my personal limitations. *(31)*
I am often my own worst enemy . . . . The temptations that Jesus faced in the wilderness were the temptations he would have the greatest difficulty resisting. *(Ch. 5, 45)*
I have made many assumptions about what I would be able to achieve. These assumptions kept me from achieving those very ends, because they negatively influenced my attitudes and actions. One of those self-defeating responses is the sense that I have lost, or never had, control of significant areas of my life. *(46)*
If I can't have things my way, I won't have them at all . . . I do not feel as though I am acting unreasonably . . . *(47)*
I like to feel sorry for myself. No one lends me sympathy quite as well as I do. *(Ch. 8, 71)*
After a setback, I am likely to set a whole new set of arbitrary and artificial limits on what I can expect to achieve. *(71)*
Most of us spend our lives trying to escape from self-centredness. Maybe that's the whole point . . . the ones who

have most success are those who somehow turn self-caring into other-caring. Faith in God implies that I am not the center of the universe. *(Ch. 4, 50)*

Suggested questions for discussion
1. Can you identify any "self-fulfilling prophecies" in your own life? Can there be good "self-fulfilling prophecies" as well as bad?
2. If miracles were possible, who do you wish you could be?
3. When you meet someone for the first time, how do you identify who you are, and what's important about you?
4. How can you know that you matter to God?
5. Do you have to earn God's love?

SESSION FOUR: MORTALITY

Purpose of session

To recognize that all of us will die someday, and to consider how that recognition might affect our current life-styles.

References

From here on it's all downhill. *(Ch. 2, 19)*

Death seldom seems just. *(Ch. 7, 61)*

The tacit acceptance that I was dying, an acceptance which I first began to reach at age fourteen, was but one step in a long journey. That journey is still in progress. *(Ch. 2, 23)*

I have had to face death many times. *(Ch. 6, 54)*

We try to avoid the reaper's apparition, at all costs, even to refusing to think about one's own death. But one can only fight so long. It is okay to die. Can't they see? It is okay to die. Can I convince myself? *(56-57)*

It's unnerving to be brought back, again and again, to stand upon the same gallows and confront the same executioner. And each time, never knowing. Do I receive another pardon, or not? *(58)*

An encounter with death is really an encounter with the whole of life. *(Ch. 7, 59)*

An encounter with death is a powerful emotional experience. I have felt fear, because death remains the great unknown. At other times, I have felt the profound sadness of saying good-byes. I am usually left with a sense of guilt . . . that I will be disappointing those people I care about most. *(60)*

Because death will ultimately absorb all my life's meanings, death needs to be approached from a perspective which grants ultimate meaning to life. *(61)*

Suggested questions for discussion

1. Have you ever thought you were going to die? How did that experience affect you?
2. Michael Schwartzentruber says "Living seems to be what I am called to do." *(Ch. 8, 69)* Does that mean ignoring death?

3. What sort of emotions would someone who is dying feel?
4. What do we fear about death?

SESSION FIVE: SEARCHING FOR FAITH

Purpose of session
To consider the role of doubt in faith, and to share ways in which we can progress towards a more mature faith.

References
My desire to be independent and self-sustaining was most evident in my struggle to find a God to whom I could relate. *(Ch. 4, 38)*

At one time, God seemed anything but loving. Any attempt to rationalize my suffering as part of God's will, left me hurt, angry and alienated. I could not love a God who, seemingly, would not love me, or would only love me while hurting me. *(Ch. 7, 62-63)*

I was determined to find the answers for myself, before I made a commitment. That attitude may reveal a common heresy in today's world, that our relationship with God depends on our initiative. That we come to God on our terms . . . *(Ch. 4, 38)*

The questions I had asked had been the biggest obstacle, not because I had asked them, but because of the way I had asked them. *(41)*

In my search for a God to whom I could be faithful, I was ultimately confronted by the absolute faithfulness of God. *(40)*

The only way to answer questions of faith is from a position of faith. God is visible most clearly to the "faithed" eye. *(41)*

If I was ever to understand God, it would not be because I had figured out God. Rather, understanding would result from God revealed in the lives and world around me. *(41)*

Suggested questions for discussion
1. Have you ever doubted the existence of God? What were some turning points that changed your mind?
2. In finding a relationship with God, what's expected of us? How much initiative do we have to take?
3. Can you believe in science and believe in God too?
4. Does God speak English? How does God communicate with us?